INTRODUCING
ISSUES WITH
OPPOSING
VIEWPOINTS®

The Effectiveness of Alternative Medicine

Lisa Idzikowski, Book Editor

GREENHAVEN
PUBLISHING

Published in 2019 by Greenhaven Publishing, LLC
353 3rd Avenue, Suite 255, New York, NY 10010

Articles in Greenhaven Publishing anthologies are often edited for length to meet page requirements. In addition, original titles of these works are changed to clearly present the main thesis and to explicitly indicate the author's opinion. Every effort is made to ensure that Greenhaven Publishing accurately reflects the original intent of the authors. Every effort has been made to trace the owners of the copyrighted material.

Library of Congress Cataloging-in-Publication Data

Names: Idzikowski, Lisa, editor.
Title: The effectiveness of alternative medicine / Lisa Idzikowski, book
  editor.
Description: First edition. | New York : Greenhaven Publishing, 2019. |
  Series: Introducing issues with opposing viewpoints | Audience: Grade
  7-12. | Includes bibliographical references and index.
Identifiers: LCCN 2018025106| ISBN 9781534504219 (library bound) | ISBN
  9781534504790 (pbk.)
Subjects: LCSH: Alternative medicine--Juvenile literature.
Classification: LCC R733 .E386 2019 | DDC 610--dc23
LC record available at https://lccn.loc.gov/2018025106

Manufactured in the United States of America

Website: http://greenhavenpublishing.com

Contents

Foreword 5

Introduction 7

Chapter 1: How Does Alternative Medicine Differ from Conventional Medical Treatment?

1. Medical Students Should Also Study Alternative Medicine 11
   Joanna Hughes
2. The Relationship Between Alternative Medicine and Western Medicine Is Contentious 16
   Deborah R. Bassett
3. We Often Don't Know if CAM Treatments Are Effective 21
   HIE Help Center
4. We Should Be Free to Manage Our Personal Health 27
   Logan Albright
5. There Are Risks to Using Natural Health Products 31
   Health Canada
6. Mainstream Medicine Should Give CAM a Chance 36
   Paul Komesaroff

Chapter 2: Does Alternative Medicine Help or Harm?

1. Alternative Medicine Is a Breeding Ground for Quackery 42
   Edzard Ernst
2. CAM May Help During Cancer Treatment 48
   Cancer Research
3. Don't Look for a Miracle Cure in Alternative Therapies 53
   Alan Levinovitz
4. There Is a Lack of Research Data on Alternative Medicine 59
   Edzard Ernst
5. We Must Consider New Ideas to Treat Diseases 63
   Scott Daniels
6. Alternative Cancer Remedies May Result in Early Death 69
   Sandra Ryan

Chapter 3: How Should the Practice of Alternative Medicine Be Changed?

1. CAM Therapies Must Undergo Rigorous Scientific Research and Testing   76
   Jon Adams

2. Industry Must Supply Funding for CAM Research   80
   Andrew Scholey

3. Stop Wasting Time and Money on Clinical Testing of Alternative Treatments   84
   Daily Mail

4. Anti-Science Sentiments Have Encouraged the Rise of Alternative Medicine   89
   Joel Gottsegen

5. The Only Treatments That Beat Cancer Are Conventional   93
   National Library of Medicine

6. Enhanced Education and Critical Thinking Skills Will Help People Reject Quackery   100
   James Randi

Facts About Alternative Medicine   108
Organizations to Contact   110
For Further Reading   113
Index   117
Picture Credits   120

Foreword

Indulging in a wide spectrum of ideas, beliefs, and perspectives is a critical cornerstone of democracy. After all, it is often debates over differences of opinion, such as whether to legalize abortion, how to treat prisoners, or when to enact the death penalty, that shape our society and drive it forward. Such diversity of thought is frequently regarded as the hallmark of a healthy and civilized culture. As the Reverend Clifford Schutjer of the First Congregational Church in Mansfield, Ohio, declared in a 2001 sermon, "Surrounding oneself with only like-minded people, restricting what we listen to or read only to what we find agreeable is irresponsible. Refusing to entertain doubts once we make up our minds is a subtle but deadly form of arrogance." With this advice in mind, Introducing Issues with Opposing Viewpoints books aim to open readers' minds to the critically divergent views that comprise our world's most important debates.

Introducing Issues with Opposing Viewpoints simplifies for students the enormous and often overwhelming mass of material now available via print and electronic media. Collected in every volume is an array of opinions that captures the essence of a particular controversy or topic. Introducing Issues with Opposing Viewpoints books embody the spirit of nineteenth-century journalist Charles A. Dana's axiom: "Fight for your opinions, but do not believe that they contain the whole truth, or the only truth." Absorbing such contrasting opinions teaches students to analyze the strength of an argument and compare it to its opposition. From this process readers can inform and strengthen their own opinions, or be exposed to new information that will change their minds. Introducing Issues with Opposing Viewpoints is a mosaic of different voices. The authors are statesmen, pundits, academics, journalists, corporations, and ordinary people who have felt compelled to share their experiences and ideas in a public forum. Their words have been collected from newspapers, journals, books, speeches, interviews, and the Internet, the fastest-growing body of opinionated material in the world.

Introducing Issues with Opposing Viewpoints shares many of the well-known features of its critically acclaimed parent series, Opposing

Viewpoints. The articles allow readers to absorb and compare divergent perspectives. Active reading questions preface each viewpoint, requiring the student to approach the material thoughtfully and carefully. Photographs, charts, and graphs supplement each article. A thorough introduction provides readers with crucial background on an issue. An annotated bibliography points the reader toward articles, books, and websites that contain additional information on the topic. An appendix of organizations to contact contains a wide variety of charities, nonprofit organizations, political groups, and private enterprises that each hold a position on the issue at hand. Finally, a comprehensive index allows readers to locate content quickly and efficiently.

Introducing Issues with Opposing Viewpoints is also significantly different from Opposing Viewpoints. As the series title implies, its presentation will help introduce students to the concept of opposing viewpoints and learn to use this material to aid in critical writing and debate. The series' four-color, accessible format makes the books attractive and inviting to readers of all levels. In addition, each viewpoint has been carefully edited to maximize a reader's understanding of the content. Short but thorough viewpoints capture the essence of an argument. A substantial, thought-provoking essay question placed at the end of each viewpoint asks the student to further investigate the issues raised in the viewpoint, compare and contrast two authors' arguments, or consider how one might go about forming an opinion on the topic at hand. Each viewpoint contains sidebars that include at-a-glance information and handy statistics. A Facts About section located in the back of the book further supplies students with relevant facts and figures.

Following in the tradition of the Opposing Viewpoints series, Greenhaven Publishing continues to provide readers with invaluable exposure to the controversial issues that shape our world. As John Stuart Mill once wrote: "The only way in which a human being can make some approach to knowing the whole of a subject is by hearing what can be said about it by persons of every variety of opinion and studying all modes in which it can be looked at by every character of mind. No wise man ever acquired his wisdom in any mode but this." It is to this principle that Introducing Issues with Opposing Viewpoints books are dedicated.

Introduction

"How has the role of a doctor changed over the years? Are there better ways to treat the kinds of health problems that can usually only be managed, not cured? And how do you gather evidence on therapies that involve not only the body but also the mind?"

—*"The Evolution of Alternative Medicine,"*
The Atlantic, June 25, 2012

According to the Mayo Clinic, complementary medicine and alternative medicine, often lumped together as CAM, are popular terms for a variety of health practices that are typically not part of conventional Western medicine. "Complementary refers to treatments that are used along with conventional medicine. And alternative treatments are those health practices used in place of conventional medicine."

The National Center for Complementary and Integrative Health, NCCIH, defines health care practices that vary from the conventional Western medical sphere as being in one of three treatment groups—complementary, alternative, or integrative. According to NCCIH, complementary health approaches include mind and body practices such as yoga, meditation, acupuncture, massage therapy, spinal manipulation, chiropractic, tai chi, qigong, relaxation techniques, healing touch and hypnotherapy. Another complementary health approach area involves the use of natural products—vitamins, minerals, herbs, and probiotics—as dietary additions. A third group of treatment practices in the complementary health approach sector includes Ayurvedic medicine, which is a traditional form of medicine long practiced in India, homeopathy, traditional healers, naturopathy, and traditional Chinese medicine. NCCIH refers to alternative medicine as those treatments totally different from and used solely in place of Western medicine, and integrative medicine as those treatments combining "conventional and CAM treatments for which there is evidence of safety and effectiveness."

In the most recent survey conducted by the Centers for Disease Control and Prevention in the United States, which gathered health information on about ninety thousand adults and seventeen thousand children, about 33 percent of adults and 12 percent of children aged 4-17 used some form of complementary health approach in the past year. Data compiled by NCCIH shows that this amounts to "about 59 million Americans" spending "money out-of-pocket on complementary health approaches" with their total spending adding up to around thirty billion dollars a year.

The United States is not alone in its use of unconventional medical practices. Around the world, non-Western medicine is often called traditional medicine (TM). In 2008 the World Health Organization (WHO) convened a meeting in Beijing, China, to discuss TM and to prepare advocacy documentation for member countries in the hope of encouraging and researching it. WHO countries adopting the Beijing Declaration endorsed a resolution which included, "a responsibility for the health of their people and should formulate national policies, regulations and standards, as part of comprehensive national health systems to ensure appropriate, safe and effective use of traditional medicine." According to information presented at the Beijing Congress, TM is almost certainly more affordable than Western medicine in developing countries, with 70 to 80 percent of the population in India and Ethiopia depending on it for primary health care. Also noted was the fact that 70 percent of Canadians, and 80 percent of Germans report using TM as complementary or alternative medical medicine.

Complementary and alternative medical treatments may be used by many people around the world, but these practices constitute a highly controversial issue with outspoken proponents and opponents. Generally, opponents argue that CAM is scientifically unsound, full of useless, untested, and untestable remedies. At best, opponents argue, CAM treatments may appear at times to provide users with positive results, but experts contend that a placebo effect is occurring in the user, not an actual cure because of the pill, or shot, or whatever treatment or practice being used. Opponents also argue that the public is being fooled by the bombardment of advertisers and celebrity endorsements insisting that whatever product being offered is authentic, and sometimes a miracle cure. An even bigger headache for medical health care providers is the concern that patients will shun conventional treatments in favor of bogus remedies. Ultimately this can lead to a worsening of disease, with shortened lifespans and possible early death for those afflicted.

Interestingly, scientific studies have proven various CAM treatments to be ineffective. In 2015, the Australian National Health and Research Council released findings on a commonly used CAM practice and found "no good quality, well-designed studies with enough participants to support the idea that homeopathy works better than a placebo or causes health improvements equal to those of another treatment." And this is only one of countless studies proving the ineffectiveness of only one type of CAM.

Proponents of complementary and alternative medicine are just as savvy and outspoken, typically maintaining that CAM is natural, has little or no side effects, and can be much less costly than conventional care. They also argue that the alternative treatments work. Well-known CAM practitioners in the United States, some of which are medically credentialed doctors, argue that the American health care system does an excellent job of curing sick people, but does a lousy job of keeping them well. Proponents maintain that patients seek alternative treatments when conventional medicine fails to help with their ills and they're looking for doctors that take time to talk.

Not surprisingly, both opponents and proponents claim to be acting in the best interest of consumers. But at the same time, individuals and groups on both sides are vocal in their opposition, going so far to claim that money, big business, or even fame is the motivating force behind treatments instead of actual health care. Clearly, alternative medicine and its effectiveness is a controversial concern. Many individuals and organized groups express strongly held opinions about complementary and alternative medicine. The current debate that surrounds the topic of alternative medicine is explored in the diverse and informative viewpoints that make up *Introducing Issues with Opposing Viewpoints: The Effectiveness of Alternative Medicine*, shedding light on this divisive and ongoing contemporary issue.

Chapter 1

How Does Alternative Medicine Differ from Conventional Medical Treatment?

Alternative medicine includes the use of herbs and natural supplements.

Medical Students Should Also Study Alternative Medicine

Joanna Hughes

"Even in cases where the jury is still out, learning about these approaches has value of its own."

In the following viewpoint Joanna Hughes analyzes the topic of non-traditional medical methods and defines the three main types of practice. Hughes argues that it is important for medical students to be schooled in alternative medicine treatments and gives examples of several medical schools that incorporate training in traditional Chinese medicine. Hughes is a full-time freelance writer and previously worked as an administrator at a research institution.

AS YOU READ, CONSIDER THE FOLLOWING QUESTIONS:

1. According to the viewpoint, what are the three non-conventional medical types?
2. Why is it important for prospective doctors to learn about alternative medicine according to the author?
3. Which non-Western type of medical treatment is being taught in some medical schools?

"Why Medical Students Should Study Alternative Medicine," by Joanna Hughes, Keystone Academic Solutions, March 13, 2017. Reprinted by permission.

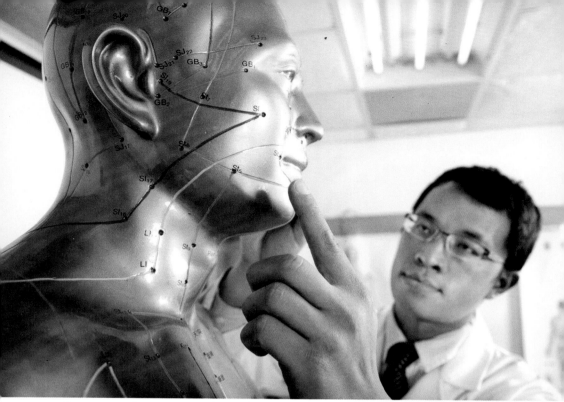

Long practiced in Eastern medicine, the focus on accupoints through accupressure and accupuncture are believed to stimulate blood circulation and promote the body's self-healing.

The term "alternative" is often used interchangeably with "complementary" and "integrative" to describe medical approaches outside of mainstream Western, AKA "conventional," medicine. However, while they all draw upon non-traditional methods, they aren't the same thing. The National Center for Complementary and Integrative Health (NCCIH) defines them as follows:

- Alternative medicine: a non-mainstream practice used in place of conventional medicine.
- Complementary medicine: a non-mainstream practice used together with conventional medicine.
- Integrative medicine: an approach that brings together conventional and complementary approaches in a coordinated way.

According to the NCCIH, "True alternative medicine is uncommon. Most people who use non-mainstream approaches use them along with conventional treatments." In other words, it's not an either/or relationship. Rather, alternative medicine — which comprises acupuncture and other traditional Chinese medicines (TCM); chiropractic medicine; energy therapies; therapeutic "healing" touch; and herbal medicine — is inextricably becoming part of the landscape of modern medicine.

Why Alternative Medicine Matters

Most patients wouldn't dream of seeing a doctor who didn't have a solid foundation in anatomy, biochemistry, pathology or pharmacology. According to a recent BMJ article, "Should Medical Students Be Taught Alternative Medicine?" the same is starting to apply to alternative medicine.

Says author Graeme Catto, "To provide quality care doctors must be aware of choices patients make and be able to discuss them in an informed and non-judgmental way. Any other approach puts the doctor-patient relationship at risk. Patients are reluctant to raise issues that they believe meet with disapproval. These principles apply to complementary and alternative medicine the same way as to other lifestyle choices."

Catto's personal experiences in the clinical setting support this conclusion: "As a nephrologist I learned that patients wanted complementary therapies to relieve some of the intractable and distressing symptoms, such as skin itch and restless legs, associated with chronic renal failure," he explains. "Patients discussed among themselves the therapies they found useful. For my part I checked that there were no known interactions with their current conventional treatment and was pleased if symptoms were relieved."

An open mindset is so important, in fact, that the UK General Medical Council's Outcomes for Graduates (Tomorrow's Doctors) includes demonstrating "awareness that many patients use complementary and alternative therapies, and awareness of the existence and range of these therapies, why patients use them, and how this might affect other types of treatment that patients are receiving" toward its overarching outcome of "mak[ing] the care of patients their first concern, applying their knowledge and skills in a competent and ethical manner and using their ability to provide leadership and to analyse complex and uncertain situations."

Mainstreaming... with a Catch

A growing body of evidence points to the benefits of alternative medicine in treating patients. For example, a recent article in the international, peer-reviewed journal Evidence-Based Complementary and Alternative Medicine (eCAM) contends, "The most rigorous method for demonstrating the effectiveness of medical interventions is the randomized controlled trial (RCT), and this has been the case for many decades. RCTs have been conducted in TCM, and some have shown very promising results such as Artemisia annua for malaria, acupuncture for low back pain, and Tai Chi for prevention of falls in the elderly."

But even in cases where the jury is still out, learning about these approaches has value of its own, according to a recent *US News & World Report* piece on the recent movement among medical schools toward alternative medicine: "Whether or not students who learn about alternative approaches ever incorporate herbs or acupuncture in their practices, believers say, they stand to gain from viewing medicine in a more holistic way."

Not only that, but where better to evaluate the safety and effectiveness of sometimes controversial alternative treatments than within an academic context? Concludes one 21st Century Oncology article, "Perhaps that very contentiousness makes research universities the natural arena for alternative medicine to respond to the challenge of science." The Irish College of Traditional Chinese Medicine's Master's Degree in Traditional Chinese Medicine, in conjunction with the Guangzhou University of Chinese Medicine, sets out to bridge this gap through the promotion of the development of higher education in the field of Chinese medicine, as well as to prepare graduates to provide quality TCM medical services to the growing number of patients seeking these treatments.

Are other schools offering students the chance to immerse themselves in a culture of holistic healing? The University of East-West

Medicine's Master of Science in Traditional Chinese Medicine (MSTCM) features an innovative curriculum that teaches traditional Chinese medicine alongside Western medical sciences while Emperor's College of Traditional Oriental Medicine works to position its graduates to be leaders in the integration of alternative medicine into modern health care.

The Indian Board of Alternative Medicines' Doctor of Medicine in Alternative Medicines M.D. (A.M.), meanwhile, is an internationally recognized holistic medicine training institute that offers distance learning coursework across a full range of alternative medicine disciplines, including naturopathy, medicinal herbalism, reflexology, acupuncture, yoga and massage, and Reiki therapy.

Still think alternative medicine has no place in the contemporary health care system? Think again. Approximately a third of Americans now look to alternative approaches for their health concerns, according to CNN. The takeaway for aspiring medical students? Studies in alternative medicine may vastly enrich your potential—and your patient base—as a doctor.

EVALUATING THE AUTHOR'S ARGUMENTS:

In this viewpoint Joanna Hughes contends that prospective medical students would be well advised to have schooling in alternative medical practices to better serve their patients, because about one in three Americans use these alternative medical services. Did the authors' argument persuade you? If so, how? If not, how could she have swayed your opinion?

Viewpoint
2

The Relationship Between Alternative Medicine and Western Medicine Is Contentious

Deborah R. Bassett

"More medical doctors and health care professionals are referring their patients to selected alternative therapies."

In the following excerpted viewpoint, Deborah R. Bassett argues that medical doctors in the United States and Canada often have negative opinions about alternative medicine. However, she notes, many are open to learning about alternative therapies that are supported by scientific research. The author outlines the differences between alternative medicine and conventional Western medicine, and concludes that a better understanding of alternative therapies is needed before conventional medical practitioners can make sound judgements. Basset conducts research and teaches communication at the University of West Florida.

Republished with permission of SAGE Publications, from "Alternative medicine. In S. Hornig Priest (Ed.), Encyclopedia of Science and Technology Communication. Thousand Oaks, CA" by Deborah R. Bassett, permission conveyed through Copyright Clearence Center, Inc.

AS YOU READ, CONSIDER THE FOLLOWING QUESTIONS:

1. According to the author, what is the strict definition of alternative medicine?
2. Identify two alternative medical therapies that US medical doctors suggest to their patients, as stated by the author.
3. What do conventional health professionals want concerning alternative medicine, according to the viewpoint?

[...]

Strictly speaking, alternative medicine refers to treatments that are used instead of conventional medicine. Complementary and alternative medicine and traditional, complementary, and alternative medicine are terms that are frequently used when discussing alternative medicine. Complementary medicine refers to therapies that are used in conjunction with mainstream treatment, while traditional medicine refers to medical practices that predate Western medicine and are still used in traditional societies in many parts of the world. Integrative medicine and holistic medicine are also terms used to refer to alternative medicine.

Conventional medicine is also referred to as allopathic medicine, mainstream medicine, Western medicine, biomedical approaches to medicine, and science-based medicine. Globally, alternative medicine refers to medical practices that fall outside the domain of mainstream Western medical practices as are used in industrialized nations such as in the United States, Canada, the United Kingdom, Australia, and Europe. Many of these practices have their origins in developing nations, such as in China or India, or among the indigenous peoples of industrialized nations, and are thus considered traditional medicine rather than alternative medicine.

[...]

Differences Between Alternative Medicine and Mainstream Medicine

Some of the key differences between alternative and mainstream medicine include the training of practitioners, the empirical basis, and the

Some argue that alternative therapies should be introduced in medical school and during medical training. Such education could reduce the animosity many medical doctors have toward alternative medicine.

choice of medical model. Mainstream medicine is practiced by medical doctors and nurses who have been trained in medical schools or colleges and who have received either a doctorate in medicine (MD), a degree in nursing such as a registered nurse (RN), or another degree such as a PhD in psychiatry. Alternative medicine practitioners do not require specific licensing, and until the early twenty-first century, there were few schools that provided accredited training for practitioners. Mainstream medicine is based on an empirical tradition of Western scientific principles. Alternative medicine is based on many different traditions, including esoteric and spiritual traditions such as Hinduism and the yin and yang philosophy of Chinese medicine.

These approaches are not considered to be scientific in the Western tradition because they have not been empirically tested and proven.

[...]

FAST FACT

About one third of Americans use some form of alternative medicine.

From the outset, the relationship between alternative medicine practitioners and traditionally trained medical doctors has been contentious. However, as a growing body of scientific research supports the effectiveness of popular alternative therapies for specific health conditions (for example, acupuncture has been shown to be successful in treating pain associated with migraines and cancer), more medical doctors and health care professionals are referring their patients to selected alternative therapies. An analysis of survey data between 1982 and 1995 suggested that many medical doctors in the United States refer their patients to popular alternative therapies including acupuncture, chiropractic treatment, and massage. The findings suggested that medical doctors are less likely, however, to refer their patients to alternative therapies for which there is not scientifically based evidence of effectiveness or that take the place of conventional medicine, such as homeopathy or herbal medicine.

Among health care professionals, there is some evidence to suggest that medical doctors in the United States and in Canada have more negative attitudes toward alternative medicine than do other health care professionals, such as nurses or pharmacists. Overall, however, conventional medicine health care professionals report that they want more information and education about alternative medicine. Studies on the perceptions of alternative medicine practitioners suggest that they appear to view their field as supporting conventional medicine, not replacing it. Although the relationship between the two sides has improved dramatically from the animosity that characterized much of the previous two centuries, there is still a need for interaction and collaboration between conventional medicine and alternative medicine providers, particularly in ensuring that patients who are being treated by both types of caregivers receive safe and effective treatment.

[...]

Conclusion

Alternative medicine continues to grow in popularity and use. [...] Rather than dismissing alternative medicine wholesale, medical doctors will need to become knowledgeable about alternative therapies to learn how to communicate effectively with their patients, many of whom are using alternative therapies.

[...]

EVALUATING THE AUTHOR'S ARGUMENTS:

In this viewpoint, Deborah R. Bassett asserts that the relationship between alternative medicine practitioners and traditionally trained medical doctors has been contentious. Why might this be so? Back up your opinion with facts from the viewpoint.

We Often Don't Know if CAM Treatments Are Effective

"CAM is positioned in opposition to what people typically consider to be 'traditional' Western medicine."

HIE Help Center

In the following viewpoint, the HIE Help Center outlines the scope of CAM and gives specific examples of CAM therapies. The authors address the controversy of whether CAM therapies are effective. The problem with this question, the authors acknowledge, is that many are not tested for efficacy. The HIE Help Center is an organization dedicated to helping and informing families of children with disabilities stemming from hypoxic-ischemic encephalopathy (HIE).

AS YOU READ, CONSIDER THE FOLLOWING QUESTIONS:
1. According to the viewpoint, what is the difference between complementary and alternative therapies?
2. Identify and gives examples of two of the five categories of CAM therapies.
3. Why might Western medical professionals be cautious about CAM therapies, according to the author?

"'Mainstream' Medicine vs. Complementary and Alternative Medicine (CAM)," HIE Help Center. Reprinted by permission.

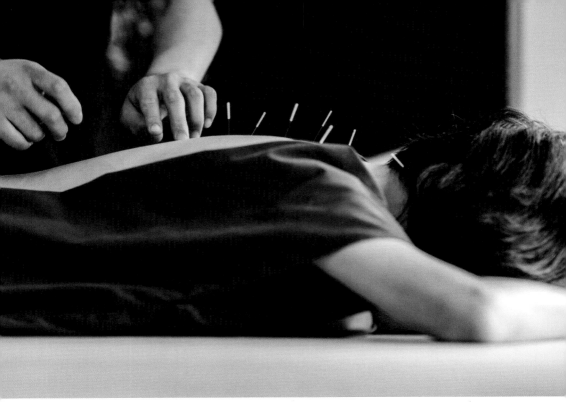

Accupuncture is one CAM therapy with a very long tradition. While many CAM therapies have not been sufficiently tested, others are accepted into mainstream medicine.

One hot topic in the treatment of children with developmental delays and disabilities is the use of complementary and alternative medicine (CAM), a collection of practices described as "outside" the scope of conventional medical practice. Because the boundaries between medicine, alternative practice, and what is considered "mainstream" treatment can be confusing, we're providing a short primer on what exactly these different terms mean.

What Is Complementary and Alternative Medicine (CAM)?

First and foremost, it's important to remember that CAM is positioned in opposition to what people typically consider to be "traditional" Western medicine. Conventional medicine is what most practitioners with MD or DO degrees practice – the focus is often on treating existing ailments within the context of very specific scientific frameworks. Treatments fall under the purview of "evidence-based medicine (EBM)," which tests different treatments to confirm that they are effective and safe. These treatments are tested in a hierarchy, with only rigorously tested procedures or treatments passing into the realm of "clinical practice guidelines."

On the other hand, CAM practices sit outside "mainstream" medicine, as they have either not been studied, not been proven to be effective, or lack scientific underpinnings to justify their inclusion in the scientific canon. It is important to note, however, that there are differences between complementary and alternative therapies:

- Complementary medicine is used in conjunction with or as a supplement to mainstream medicine.
- Alternative therapies are used to replace mainstream medical solutions, and thus may often carry with them correspondingly greater risks.

It is also very important to note that what is considered CAM can sometimes be a moving target because sometimes CAM therapies do get rigorously tested and adopted into "regular" medicine. Some doctors, due to very high demand, even combine CAM practices with mainstream medicine in a hybrid called integrative medicine. One common rebuttal to CAM is, "If it were proven to work, it wouldn't be an 'alternative treatment' – we'd all be using them."

According to the National Center for Complementary and Integrative Health (NCCIH, formerly NCCAM), these therapies can be divided into five different categories:

- Alternative medical systems (medical treatments that center on specific philosophy, such as Ayurveda, first Nations traditional healing, traditional Chinese medicine, homeopathy and naturopathy)
- Mind-body interventions (treatments that involve fostering the mind-body connection, such as meditation, prayer, relaxation, and art therapy)
- Biologically based therapies (such as dietary supplements and herbal remedies)
- Manipulative and body-based methods (such as chiropractic and osteopathic manipulation and massage)
- Energy therapies (such as biofield therapies – including qigong,

therapeutic touch, and Reiki – and bioelectromagnetic-based therapies such as magnet therapy or alternating-current or direct-current field therapy)

In many cases, however, there is a great deal of overlap, and the division between many of these therapies is not clear-cut. Many of these therapies claim to focus on the individual "holistically," looking to improve physical, emotional, mental, and spiritual health.

Some medical practitioners can be cautious regarding recommending CAM therapies because many (if not most) have not undergone rigorous testing to confirm their safety. Some CAM therapies (such as dietary supplementation for cancer treatment) have been found not only ineffective but actively harmful.

Is CAM Effective?

It is not possible to say that CAM therapies as a whole are ineffective, however, as many have not been tested for efficacy. Very controlled trials are expensive, which can make CAM efficacy testing difficult. Conventional medicine research is often supported by private firms, so clinical trials are feasible for them. CAM generally doesn't have the same kind of backing, so clinical trials are more difficult to carry out. It is important to note, however, that without rigorous tests, it is very difficult to know what the possible risks and benefits of a CAM therapy could be. While some clinical trials for CAMs demonstrate some benefits, the benefits do not pass the standards for controlled clinical trials. Because of this, parents should exercise caution and talk to a medical professional to help make informed decisions if you are considering CAM therapies.

How CAM Therapies Are Tested for Efficacy

To demonstrate that CAM therapies are effective, there are three "tiers" of support for their use. The most rigorous is a demonstration of clinical outcomes through controlled clinical trials. Less rigorous is a demonstration of established physiological mechanisms of action (i.e., demonstrating that a treatment has an effect on some specific process that occurs in the body). The least persuasive is historical use, though this is generally considered anecdotal and unreliable evidence.

In many cases, CAM is not practiced in a culture of evidence-based medicine, however, so disproving efficacy is not always enough to discourage the use of ineffective therapies.

Before Trying a Complementary or Alternative Therapy

Before trying an alternative therapy, remember that doctors are trained and licensed. CAM practitioners often don't have to be, and many are not. Many health professionals recommend asking a health care provider such as a primary care physician for a referral if you are interested in CAM services, gathering information about the practitioner, and asking about the pros and cons of treatment – just like you would with any other medical care provider.

Examples of Complementary and Alternative Therapy

What are examples of Complementary and Alternative Medicine (CAM)?

- Acupuncture
- Alexander technique
- Aromatherapy
- Ayurveda
- Biofeedback
- Chiropractic medicine
- Diet therapy
- Herbalism
- Holistic nursing
- Homeopathy
- Hypnosis
- Massage therapy
- Meditation
- Naturopathy
- Nutritional therapy
- Osteopathic manipulative therapy (OMT)

- Qigong (internal and external qigong)
- Reflexology
- Reiki
- Spiritual healing
- Tai Chi
- Traditional Chinese medicine (TCM)
- Yoga

EVALUATING THE AUTHOR'S ARGUMENTS:

In this viewpoint, the HIE Help Center provides of list of CAM therapies and also briefly outlines the controversy of whether these therapies are effective. Do all CAM therapies need to be rigorously tested? Why or why not?

We Should Be Free to Manage Our Personal Health

"It is arrogant to assume that a central authority can always know the best treatment for a patient."

Logan Albright

In the following viewpoint, Logan Albright argues that, regardless of the efficacy of alternative medical treatments, we should be free to choose the treatments we want. The author criticizes what he sees as overreach in government regulation when it comes to the medicine we take. If we are at liberty to decline treatment, then why should we be forbidden from pursuing alternative therapies, he asks. The truth is, the author argues, doctors and scientists don't know everything when it comes to medical treatment and disease. Albright is a writer and economist in Washington, DC.

AS YOU READ, CONSIDER THE FOLLOWING QUESTIONS:

1. What particular branch of alternative medicine does the author consider "an outright fraud"?
2. How does the author feel personally about alternative medicine's efficacy?
3. What does the author assert about children's medical care?

Who should decide whether chiropracty is an effective treatement or pseudoscience? If some patients believe it works for them, isn't that enough?

Alternative medicine has been a popular target of late for the ongoing "which party is more anti-science" debate. While Republicans are derided for not buying into global warming or evolution, Democrats are attracting an equal amount of ridicule for their stances on GMOs, vaccines and, yes, alternative medicine.

I am not here to defend alternative medicine. It seems ridiculous to me that taking massive amounts of dietary supplements in pill form can be good for one's health and I have long considered chiropractic an outright fraud. But I am troubled by the desire in some circles to take the power of medical choice away from patients and put it into the hands of judges and other designated experts.

Yes, many alternative treatments are fraudulent or downright dangerous, but the argument for letting a judge decide what treatments you can and can't have is equally dangerous. It is not difficult to find a licensed physician willing to administer an unsafe and ineffective alternative treatments. Indeed, if you are a licensed chiropractor, you're perfectly free to break babies' necks! The authority vested in these people by the state does not guarantee infallibility, or even competence. Greater authoritarianism in medicine will not eliminate bad doctors, it will just eliminate the freedom of the consumer to choose.

We know from firsthand testimony that some people really are helped by alternative treatments, and whether it be real or simply the placebo effect is largely irrelevant as long as the patient gets relief. The state has no business denying people the opportunity to pursue the treatments they believe to have the best chance of helping them. Suppose all forms of conventional medicine have already been tried; does it then make since to forbid patients from trying alternative solutions, to legally compel them to sit quietly and wait for death?

Speaking of waiting for death, it should be noted that there is no law against sick people declining treatment altogether. If I develop cancer and choose to do nothing, I am permitted to do so. Why then, should I be prevented from trying an unconventional therapy that might actually help me?

It is arrogant to assume that a central authority can always know the best treatment for a patient. Every body is different, and our medical knowledge is still far from complete. There is every possibility that certain treatments being administered now are actually harmful, just as those from the past have been discredited. Do we really want to be in the position of mandating by law treatments that may prove deadly in the future?

The case of children is, of course, more difficult. Lawmakers have long grappled with the tension between religious freedom and child abuse when Christian Scientists or Jehovah's Witnesses refuse to allow their children to be treated for easily curable diseases. Since children cannot give informed consent, someone has to make these decisions for them; the question is whether the government is in a

> ## FAST FACT
>
> According to the American Chiropractic Association, chiropractors treat more than 35 million Americans annually. Chiropractors are required to pass national board exams and to be licensed by the state in which they practice.

better position to make this decision than the parents themselves.

It is my personal opinion that when in doubt, it is better to defer to the parents' wishes, since they know the individual circumstances of their child better than any government bureaucrat ever could.

By all means, physicians should try to reason with people, present them with the evidence and explain to them the dangers of the alternatives, but ultimately the choice must be left to the patient, or if that is not possible, with the patient's family.

Personal health is just that – personal, and people should be free to make their own decisions on how to manage it. The downside of that is that some people will be duped into treatments that don't work – laws against fraud and malpractice exist to try to limit the extent to which this happens, and they should be fully utilized to keep wrongdoers in check. However, the benefits of freedom are greater still. As a patient, you have the right to control your own life, and your health care decisions should not rest solely in the hands of mid-level civil servants. To put a slightly different connotation on a familiar proverb: if you don't have your health, you don't have anything.

EVALUATING THE AUTHOR'S ARGUMENTS:

Viewpoint author Logan Albright approaches the topic of CAM from a place of personal liberty rather than arguing for or against the merits of alternative medicine. Does this perspective affect your ideas about alternative medicine? If so, how?

There Are Risks to Using Natural Health Products

"Natural health products (NHPs) are naturally occurring substances that are used to restore or maintain good health."

Health Canada

In the following viewpoint, Health Canada analyzes the natural health products, or NHPs, that are used by Canadians. The author admits there are risks to using these products but informs users of the process undergone to analyze and then rate products that are safe and effective. Health Canada advises consumers of ways to protect themselves against potential risks and side effects—advice that can be used by any consumers, not just Canadians. Health Canada is an institution dedicated to helping Canadians improve and maintain their health.

AS YOU READ, CONSIDER THE FOLLOWING QUESTIONS:
1. According to the viewpoint, what is the definition of NHPs?
2. What are three risks of NHPs, as stated by the author?
3. Identify three risk prevention strategies for NHP use as reported by Health Canada.

Just because an herb or supplement is natural does not mean it is always safe. These remedies are not regulated as prescription medicines are.

Using natural health products can be a good way to maintain or improve your health. But just because a product is "natural" doesn't mean it is safe for you to use.

What Are Natural Health Products?

Natural health products (NHPs) are naturally occurring substances that are used to restore or maintain good health. They are often made from plants but can also be made from animals, microorganisms, and marine sources. They come in a wide variety of forms like tablets, capsules, tinctures, solutions, creams, ointments, and drops.

Natural health products, often called "complementary" or "alternative" medicines, include:

- Vitamins and minerals
- Herbal remedies
- Homeopathic medicines

- Traditional medicines like traditional Chinese and Ayurvedic (East Indian) medicines
- Probiotics
- Other products like amino acids and essential fatty acids

Many everyday consumer products, like certain toothpastes, antiperspirants, shampoos, facial products, and mouthwashes are also classified as natural health products in Canada.

Fast fact: 71 percent of Canadians have used natural health products like vitamins and minerals, herbal products, and homeopathic medicines.

NHPs are used and marketed for a number of health reasons, like the prevention or treatment of an illness or condition, the reduction of health risks, or the maintenance of good health. They must be safe to be used as over-the-counter products. Products needing a prescription are regulated as drugs.

Are There Risks to Using Natural Health Products?

While natural health products are generally safe and have fewer side effects than medications, they are not risk-free. Risks include:

- Manufacturing problems (like contamination, incorrect ingredients or dosage)
- Unproven claims, which can lead people to use the wrong products for serious conditions or to delay proper treatment
- Not enough information for people to make an informed choice (like incorrect instructions or no warnings that a product may not be suitable for certain groups)
- Interaction with prescription drugs or other natural health products
- Unwanted side effects, like allergic reactions

Fast fact: 12 percent of Canadians who use natural health products report that they have experienced unwanted side effects (adverse reactions).

Health Canada responded to Canadians' concerns about these risks by creating the Natural Health Products Regulations in 2004. See *What is Health Canada doing to Protect Me?* for more.

How Can I Use Natural Health Products Safely?

Take these steps to minimize your risk:

- Talk to a health care professional like a doctor, pharmacist, or naturopath before choosing a product. This is especially important for children, pregnant or breastfeeding women, seniors, and people with serious medical conditions.
- To prevent interactions, make sure your health care provider knows what other drugs and natural health products you are using.
- Use approved products. Look for NPN / DIN-HM numbers that identify licensed products.
- Be skeptical of health-related claims that seem too good to be true. Don't rely on ads: do your own research and talk to your health care provider.
- Read and follow all instructions on the product label.
- Report unwanted side effects (adverse reactions) to your health care provider and Health Canada.

How Do I Know if a Product Has Been Authorized?

To be licensed in Canada, natural health products must be safe, effective, of high quality and carry detailed label information to let people make safe and informed choices.

You can identify products that have been licensed for sale in Canada by looking for the eight-digit Natural Product Number (NPN) or Homeopathic Medicine Number (DIN-HM) on the label.

A NPN or DIN-HM means that the product has been authorized for sale in Canada and is safe and effective when used according the instructions on the label.

You can search for licensed natural health products using Health Canada's Licensed Natural Health Products Database.

How Do I Report Unwanted Side Effects?

You should report unwanted side effects (adverse reactions) to your health care provider and to Health Canada.

Reporting side effects is important because it helps Health Canada identify rare or serious adverse reactions, make changes in product safety information, issue public warnings and advisories, and/or remove unsafe products from the Canadian market.

Fast fact: Only 41 percent of Canadians who experienced unwanted side effects (adverse reactions) to natural health products reported them.

What Is Health Canada Doing to Protect Me?

Health Canada ensures that all Canadians have ready access to a wide range of natural health products that are safe, effective, and of high quality.

We assess all natural health products before letting them be sold in Canada. We also ensure they are properly manufactured (without contamination or incorrect ingredients). And we do post-market monitoring to make sure that NHP Regulations are being followed.

EVALUATING THE AUTHOR'S ARGUMENTS:

In this viewpoint, Health Canada reports on the topic of natural health products and provides risks and reasons why Canadians can trust these products. Why might users not consider risks when it comes to natural products?

Viewpoint 6

Mainstream Medicine Should Give CAM a Chance

Paul Komesaroff

"It's about opening up possibilities, not closing them down."

In the following viewpoint, Paul Komesaroff argues that both complementary and Western medicine should benefit from funding and research. The author opens by reminding the reader that there was a time when Western medicine was not considered legitimate, much like CAM therapies today. He suggests that research and testing of alternative medicine should be allowed to be conducted in universities, as they are exactly where new and unpopular ideas should be examined. Komesaroff is a professor of medicine at Monash University.

AS YOU READ, CONSIDER THE FOLLOWING QUESTIONS:

1. During what century was modern medicine formed, according to the viewpoint?
2. What is the name of the group mentioned by the author that formed to counter pseudoscience in medicine?
3. According to the author, in what key places is science conducted?

Modern medicine is the result of years of trial and error and evolving beliefs among the scientific community. In 100 years CAM might be accepted into the mainstream.

Medicine has long been the subject of vigorous debate about the control of social resources. The formation of modern medicine in the mid-19th century was itself the result of a century-long fight for legitimacy among many contending groups. At that time, those who won out – the physicians, the surgeons and those who prepared and sold medicines – had no more evidence to support them than those they defeated. They succeeded on the basis of politics, not of evidence.

Since then, Western medicine has grown into a key social institution supported by an elaborate scientific infrastructure. But the battle to defend its status, authority, and access to wealth continues unabated.

On the one hand, doctors and their professional organizations are engaged in regular disputes with government about the control of fees and budgets, disciplinary practices and accreditation, and the extent of their decision-making power. On the other hand, there is a persistent need to defend the boundaries against opposing forms of health care – so-called complementary medicine. The latter haven't died out, despite the undisputed success of medicine. Indeed, estimates show that in most developed countries, including Australia, about half the population regularly use health practices outside the mainstream.

By and large, most people would agree that this is unproblematic and regard it as just part of the rough and tumble of democratic life. What's more, the current arrangements are regarded as broadly satisfactory. The ability of individuals to choose their own forms of health care is maintained, subject to some limits on what practitioners can do: in the case of complementary therapists, for example, there are rules – admittedly, not always enforced – to protect vulnerable people from unscrupulous, unfounded, and dangerous practices and restrictions on the kinds of claims that can be made in advertising and promotional materials.

Western Vs. Complementary Medicine

Debates about complementary medicine's place in society have traditionally been vigorous, but reasoned, with the proponents of medicine calling on the authority of science, and their opponents either appealing to their own evidence, which may be derived from traditional practices, or to philosophical theories, or drawing attention to perceived limitations of Western medicine.

But there is a current tendency in Australia that may have crossed the line from reasoned discussion to the inappropriate use of power and authority. A group referring to itself as the Friends of Science in Medicine, made up of senior doctors and scientists, has set itself up to "counter the growth" of what it regards as "pseudoscience in medicine", where "true science" is defined as a set of practices characterised by "an experimental, evidence-based approach."

The strategy of the group is to apply pressure on government and educational institutions through advertisements, the use of the media, and sometimes personal criticisms of individuals to withdraw or prohibit funding for complementary health practices. The organization models itself on groups in the United States and the United Kingdom that have succeeded in having funding removed from certain "alternative medicine" courses.

Philosophically and ethically, the approach of the group is questionable. As any practitioner knows, the role of empirical evidence in determining a particular clinical decision is, at best, partial and tentative. What we do is pose hypotheses on the basis of laboratory or clinical studies, which we then test through careful observation and assessment of outcomes. Each decision is conditioned by the unique circumstances of the individual involved, including his or her personal medical history, goals, values, and preferences. It's about opening up possibilities, not closing them down.

The Role of Universities

The key places in our society where science is conducted are the universities. These should therefore be protected as sites where unpopular ideas and theories can be examined. They must foster criticisms of orthodoxy, especially those embedded in the institutions of power and authority. Both Western medical practitioners and scientists – like myself – and their interlocutors must be challenged and called to account for their claims and judgments.

What is objectionable about Friends of Science in Medicine is their lack of respect for the fragile balance on which genuine dialogues about knowledge and ethics depend, and their readiness to resort to the use of power and authority to win an intellectual debate. Of course, the medical research and teaching budgets are in the hundreds of millions of dollars, so the power is on their side. Although they may therefore win the battle, the trouble is that control of wealth and the institutions of authority does not generate truth.

Clear Thinking

None of this means that there are not problems, either with complementary medicines or with aspects of Western medicine. In both cases, vulnerable members of the community need to be protected from exaggerated or misleading claims. In both cases, the evidence – in all its forms – needs to be scrutinized and presented clearly and fairly to patients. And in both cases, the process of communication has to be open, respectful, and free of contamination with power or self-interest.

In the spirit and tradition of science, if there is a disagreement, let it be resolved in the crucible of public discourse. We do not need intellectual vigilantes patroling the corridors of our institutions looking for theories or ideas with which they disagree to drive them out from our midst.

EVALUATING THE AUTHOR'S ARGUMENTS:

Viewpoint author Paul Komesaroff argues in favor of open minds rather than supporting one form of medicine over another. Does this perspective change whatever opinions you had about alternative medicine? Point to passages in the viewpoint that changed your mind—or that were ineffective in changing your mind.

Chapter 2

Does Alternative Medicine Help or Harm?

Not all alternative therapies are as accepted or as benign as the practice of yoga.

Alternative Medicine Is a Breeding Ground for Quackery

Edzard Ernst

"'Quack' is often employed as a disrespectful description for clinicians, particularly those who are unskilled and employ bogus therapies for a profit."

In the following viewpoint, Edzard Ernst provides strategies that patients can use to protect themselves from quacks masquerading as alternative medical practitioners. Ernst argues that alternative medicine is ripe with quackery and he details scenarios that quacks use to fool patients into believing that they are receiving bona fide medical treatments. Edzard Ernst is a professor emeritus at the University of Exeter and was awarded the John Maddox Prize in 2015 for standing up for science.

AS YOU READ, CONSIDER THE FOLLOWING QUESTIONS:

1. What is a nonexisting diagnosis according to Ernst?
2. As outlined by the author, what are two ways that quacks fool patients?
3. As explained by the author, which human body organs work as detoxification agents?

"Six signs you are being treated by a quack," by Edzard Ernst, The Spectator (1828) Ltd, August 5, 2016. Reprinted by permission.

Just as with medical doctors it is a good idea to research alternative therapy practitioners and their treatments before giving them your money and entrusting your body to them.

The term "quack" is often employed as a disrespectful description for clinicians, particularly those who are unskilled, ignorant, dishonest, and employ bogus therapies for a profit. Quacks are everywhere, I am afraid, but alternative medicine seems like a promised land to them. Quackery endangers our wealth and, more importantly, our health.

To protect yourself from quackery, it is essential to be able to recognise the quacks' "tricks of the trade" and to take appropriate action against them. In this two-part article, I will disclose some of the most popular ploys used by quacks operating in the realm of alternative medicine, and I will offer some advice on quackery prevention.

Treating Nonexistent Conditions

There is nothing better for enhancing a quack's cash flow than allowing him to treat a condition that does not exist. Many alternative practitioners have made a true cult of this handy option. Go to a chiropractor and you will, in all likelihood, receive a diagnosis of "subluxation"; consult a practitioner of traditional Chinese medicine and you might be diagnosed as suffering from "chi deficiency"; see a homeopath and he might tell you that your "vital force" needs boosting.

The beauty of a nonexisting diagnosis is that the practitioner can treat it, and treat it, and treat it…until the client has run out of money or patience. Just before this point, however, the practitioner would proudly inform you that "you are completely healthy now." This happens to be true, of course, because you have been healthy all along.

My advice for avoiding such exploitation: make sure that the diagnosis given by someone you suspect of quackery is correct; if necessary consult a real health care professional.

It Must Get Worse Before It Gets Better

When, after receiving regular treatments, patients feel not better but worse, quacks tend to tell them that this is entirely normal — because things have to get worse before they get better. They call this a "healing crisis." But the healing crisis is a phenomenon for which no compelling evidence has ever been produced.

Imagine a patient with moderately severe symptoms consulting a clinician and receiving treatment. There are only three things that can happen to her:

- She can get better.
- She might experience no change at all.
- She might get worse.

In the first scenario, the practitioner would obviously claim that his therapy caused the improvement. In the second scenario, he might say that without his therapy, symptoms would have deteriorated. In the third scenario, a quack would tell his patient that she is experiencing a healing crisis. In other words, the myth of the healing crisis is little more than a trick of the trade to make patients continue supporting the quack's livelihood.

My advice: when you hear the term "healing crisis," go and find a real doctor to help you with your condition.

A Cure Takes a Long Time

But there are other ploys to deal with patients who fail to improve after long-term therapy. Let's assume your problem is back pain, and that the pain has not eased despite numerous treatments and large amounts of money spent. Surely in such a situation you would call it a day. You will have had enough. And this would, of course, be a serious threat to the quack's cash flow.

To avert the shortfall, the practitioner merely has to explain that your condition has been going on for a very long time (if this happens not to be true, the practitioner would explain that the pain might be relatively recent but the underlying condition is chronic). Naturally, this means that a cure will also have to take a very long time — after all, Rome was not built in one day!

The continuation of ineffective treatments despite the absence of any improvement is usually not justifiable on medical grounds. It is, however, entirely justifiable on the basis of financial considerations: quacks rely on their patients' regular payments and will therefore think of all sorts of means to achieve this aim.

My advice is to see a clinician who can help you within a reasonable and predictable amount of time. Insist on a proper treatment plan from the outset and stop if it is not fulfilled.

Thinking Holistically

The notion that alternative medicine takes care of the whole person attracts many consumers. Never mind that nothing could be further from being holistic than, for instance, diagnosing conditions by looking at a patient's iris (iridology), or focussing on her spine (chiropractic, osteopathy), or massaging the soles of her feet (reflexology). And never mind that any type of good conventional medicine is by definition holistic. What counts is the label, and "holistic" is a most desirable one indeed. Nothing sells quackery better than holism.

Most quacks rub their false holism into the minds of their patients whenever and however they can. It has the added advantage that they have seemingly plausible excuses for their therapeutic failures. Imagine a patient consulting a practitioner with depression and, even after prolonged treatment, her condition is unchanged.

In such a situation, quacks do not need to despair: they will point out that they never treat diagnostic labels but always the whole person. Therefore, the patient's depression might not have changed, but surely other issues have improved…and, if the patient introspects hard enough, she might find that her appetite has improved, that her indigestion is better, or that her tennis elbow is less painful (given enough time, things do change). The holism of quacks may be a false pretence, but its benefits for a quack's income are undeniable.

My advice: take holism from quacks with more than a pinch of salt.

Detoxification

Many quacks surprise their patients by informing them that they are being poisoned. Subsequently, they insist that they need to detox and, as it happens, their type of treatment is ideally suited to achieve this aim. Detox is short for detoxification which, in real medicine, is the term used for weaning addicts off their drugs. In alternative medicine, however, the term has become a marketing tool devoid of any medical sense.

The poisons in question are never accurately defined. Instead, you will hear vague terminologies such as metabolic waste products or environmental toxins. The reason for that lack of precision is simple: once the poison is named, we would be able to measure it and test the efficacy of the treatment in question in eliminating it from the body. But this is the last thing quacks want — because it would soon establish how bogus their claims really are.

None of the alternative therapies claimed to detox your body do, in fact, eliminate any toxin; all they do take from us is our cash.

Your body has organs (skin, lungs, kidneys, liver) which take care of most of the toxins you are exposed to. If any of these organs fail, you do not need homeopathic globuli, detoxifying diets, or electric foot baths, or any other charlatanry; in this case, you are more likely to need intensive care in an A&E department.

My advice is, as soon as you hear the word "detox" from an alternative practitioner, ask for your money back and go home.

The Test of Time

Many alternative therapies have been around for hundreds if not thousands of years. To the quacks, this fact means that these interventions have "stood the test of time." They argue that acupuncture, for instance, would not be in use anymore, if it were not effective. For them, the age of their therapy is like a badge of approval from millions of people before us, a badge that surely weighs more than any amount of scientific studies.

But let's get real: we are talking of technologies, of course, health technologies, in fact. Would we argue that a hot air balloon is an older technology than an airplane and therefore better suited for transporting people from A to B?

The fact that acupuncture or any other alternative therapy was developed many centuries ago might just indicate that it was invented by people who understood too little about the human body to come up with a truly effective intervention. And the fact that blood-letting was used for centuries (and thus killed millions) should teach us a lesson about the true value of "the test of time" in medicine.

My advice is to offer leeches, blood-letting, and mercury cures to the quacks who try to persuade you that the "test of time" proves anything about the value of their quackery.

EVALUATING THE AUTHOR'S ARGUMENTS:

In this viewpoint, Edzard Ernst explains the ways that quacks fool patients into believing that they are receiving bona fide medical treatment. Choose a side and construct an argument either for or against the alternative treatments outlined in this viewpoint.

CAM May Help During Cancer Treatment

"There is growing evidence that certain complementary therapies can help to control some symptoms of cancer and treatment side effects."

Cancer Research

In the following viewpoint, authors from Cancer Research maintain that there is little research evidence that complementary therapies help with the adverse side effects of cancer or its treatment. Nonetheless, patients use these therapies in a number of ways, and evidence is growing to show that people are experiencing some positive effects during the course of their illness. While some alternative therapies can pose dangerous threats, others may be successful, particularly when patients have run out of options. Cancer Research is a registered charity in the United Kingdom.

AS YOU READ, CONSIDER THE FOLLOWING QUESTIONS:
1. Why do people use complementary therapy during cancer treatment, according to the author?
2. What is a negative effect of natural healing therapy as reported by Cancer Research?
3. According to Cancer Research, what might health practitioners like about complementary therapy?

Complementary and alternative therapies can be effective as supplements to cancer treatment.

There are a number of reasons why people use complementary or alternative therapies.

An overview of studies (a meta analysis) published in 2012 suggested that around half of people with cancer use some sort of complementary therapy at some time during their illness.

There is no evidence to suggest that any type of complementary therapy prevents or cures cancer.

For some therapies there is currently very little research evidence to show that they help with certain symptoms – for example, pain or hot flushes.

But there is research going on and we are starting to collect evidence for some types of therapy.

Using Therapies to Help You Feel Better

People often use complementary therapies to help them feel better and cope with having cancer and treatment. How you feel plays a part in how you cope.

Many complementary therapies concentrate on relaxation and reducing stress. They might help to calm your emotions, relieve anxiety, and increase your general sense of health and well-being.

Many doctors, cancer nurses, and researchers are interested in the idea that positive emotions can improve your health.

Reducing Symptoms or Side Effects

There is growing evidence that certain complementary therapies can help to control some symptoms of cancer and treatment side effects.

For example, acupuncture can help to relieve sickness caused by some chemotherapy drugs. Or, it can help relieve a sore mouth after having treatment for head and neck cancer.

Acupuncture can also help to relieve pain after surgery to remove lymph nodes in the neck.

Feeling More in Control

Sometimes it might feel as though your doctor makes many of the decisions about your treatment. It can feel like you don't have much control over what happens to you.

Many people say complementary therapy lets them take a more active role in their treatment and recovery, in partnership with their therapist.

Natural and Healing Therapies

Many patients like the idea that complementary therapies seem natural and nontoxic.

Some complementary therapies can help with specific symptoms or side effects. But we don't know much about how they might interact with conventional treatments like cancer drugs or radiotherapy.

And some types of complementary or alternative medicine might make conventional treatment work less well. And some might increase side effects.

Comfort from Touch, Talk and Time

Some people might get a lot of comfort and satisfaction from the touch, talk and time that a complementary therapist usually offers.

A good therapist can play a supportive role during cancer treatment and recovery. For example, a skilled and caring aromatherapist can take the time to make you feel cared for. This might help improve your quality of life.

Staying Positive

Having a positive outlook is an important part of coping with cancer for most people. It is normal to want and hope for a cure, even if your doctor suggests that this might be difficult.

Some people use complementary therapies as a way to feel positive and hopeful for the future.

Boosting Your Immune System

There are claims that certain complementary therapies can boost the immune system and help fight cancer. There is evidence that feeling good and reducing stress boosts the immune system. But doctors don't know if this can help the body to control cancer.

There are clinical trials looking at how certain complementary therapies might affect the immune system.

Looking for a Cure

Some people believe that using specific alternative therapies instead of conventional cancer treatment might help control or cure their cancer. There are also people who promote alternative therapies in this way.

Using alternative therapy can become more important to people with advanced cancer if their conventional treatment is no longer helping to control it. It is understandable that they hope that alternative therapies might work.

But, there is no scientific evidence to prove that any type of alternative therapy can help to control or cure cancer. Some alternative therapies might be unsafe and can cause harmful side effects.

EVALUATING THE AUTHOR'S ARGUMENTS:

In this viewpoint, Cancer Research analyzes how complementary therapy may be a positive part of cancer treatment. What concerns, and cautions, does Cancer Research see in complementary therapy? Give specific examples from the viewpoint.

Don't Look for a Miracle Cure in Alternative Therapies

"Withdrawal from false hope has a silver lining: it allows you to start looking for real hope."

Alan Levinovitz

In the following excerpted viewpoint, Alan Levinovitz shares personal experiences from two medical doctors and their family's struggle with the treatment of two sons with autism. Levinovitz details the hope that the Laidlers at first put into alternative treatments and the struggles they eventually encountered when they realized that alternative treatments would not be effective. In the end Levinovitz outlines what did work, and how the Laidler family moved beyond hoping for a cure that would not appear. Levinovitz is a professor at James Madison University in Virginia, and his writing appears in many popular sites and academic venues.

AS YOU READ, CONSIDER THE FOLLOWING QUESTIONS:
1. What event turned the Laidlers away from alternative therapies according to Levinovitz?
2. How do proponents of alternative therapies argue for their case as stated in the viewpoint?
3. What solution did the Laidlers take with their son, as reported by the author?

"An Alternative-Medicine Believer's Journey Back to Science," by Alan Levinovitz, Condé Nast, April 29, 2015. Reprinted by permission.

Parents desperate to help their sick children can be blinded by the vague promises of alternative therapies. It can be difficult to think critically and scientifically when emotions are high.

Jim and Louise Laidler lost their faith on a trip to Disneyland in 2002, while having breakfast in Goofy's Kitchen.

The Laidlers are doctors, and their sons, Ben and David, had been diagnosed with autism. For several years, on the advice of doctors and parents, the Laidlers treated their children with a wide range of alternative medicine techniques designed to stem or even reverse autistic symptoms. They gave their boys regular supplements of vitamin B12, magnesium, and dimethylglycine. They kept David's diet free of gluten and casein, heeding the advice of experts who warned that even the smallest bit of gluten would cause severe regression. They administered intravenous infusions of secretin, said to have astonishing therapeutic effects for a high percentage of autistic children.

[...]

It was in the grip of these doubts when, inside Goofy's Kitchen, Jim and Louise returned to their table from the buffet and noticed 6-year-old David hadn't come with them. They saw him standing at the buffet, devouring a waffle. The Laidlers feared the worst. "We'd been told that the slightest smidgen of gluten would crash him," Jim says. "It was absolutely devastating to watch." But by the end of the vacation, they realized David was fine. Nothing happened.

When they returned home, the Laidlers took David off his restrictive diet, and he continued to improve—rapidly. Louise stopped Ben's supplement regimen—without telling Jim—and Ben's behavior remained the same. Then, after months of soul-searching, Jim Laider took to the internet to announce his "de-conversion" from alternative medicine—a kind of penance, but also a warning to others. "I had this guilt to expunge," Jim says. "I helped to promote this nonsense, and I didn't want other people to fall for it like I did."

The Laidlers' story is a microcosm of the changing debate over so-called alternative medicine and its cousin, integrative medicine. In 2007, Americans spent $2.9 billion on homeopathic medicine, a treatment based on the belief that minuscule amounts of what causes symptoms in a healthy person will alleviate symptoms in someone who is ill. From nutritional supplements to energy healing to acupuncture, treatments outside the medical mainstream are big business. But the vast majority of scientists find much of alternative medicine highly problematic.

[...]

When Jim Laidler became an alt-medicine apostate, proponents of the treatments he criticized went on the attack. He received death threats from parents. It's an intellectually and emotionally bruising battle no matter which side you're on, one that today pits not just doctor against layperson, but also doctor against doctor. And as the Laidlers demonstrate, it can pit well-trained doctors against their own psyche. "I was happier because we felt like we were doing something right," Jim Laidler says of the treatments he gave his sons over the course of so many years. "That's how the madness begins. You want to believe that it's working, so you force yourself to see results, and silence the scientific part of your brain."

[...]

The Alternative
Whenever mainstream medicine has little to offer, other sources offer a dizzying array of options. Call it a market for hope. Autism, ALS,

FAST FACT

A published data analysis in 2018 in the *Journal of the American Medical Association* indicates that 1 in 41 children are diagnosed with autism.

Alzheimer's, terminal cancer. There's no shortage of claims that these intractable conditions can be treated using approaches that conventional Western physicians fail to consider.

Loosely categorized as "alternative medicine," the approaches include nutritional supplements, dietary regimens, detoxification protocols, acupuncture, energy healing, homeopathy, chiropractic, traditional Indian medicine, and whatever else has anecdotal support yet remains unaccepted by the larger scientific community.

Proponents of alternative healing modalities argue that the medical industrial complex willfully ignores natural, holistic approaches to health care, choosing instead to pursue more profitable treatments such as surgery and pharmaceuticals, treating symptoms and ignoring the cause to ensure that patients return for more procedures and prescriptions. New medical paradigms threaten this status quo, these voices say, so universities keep their students ignorant of powerful therapies. There are miraculous treatments available—but only if you're willing to look outside the hospital.

[…]

"I Never Run Out of Options"

Twenty years later, belief in the power of alternative therapies is not uncommon—even at the highest levels of medicine. When the Laidlers first embraced alternative practices, it was largely separate from mainstream hospitals and medical schools, but integrative medicine has changed that.

At Yale, physician and prominent health advocate David Katz practices integrative medicine, aiming to combine acceptance of alternative treatments with scientific rigor and regulation. Katz opposes chelation, along with all non-standard protocols proven to be physically harmful, but he supports being open-minded about many other alternative techniques, including acupuncture, homeopathy, and Reiki.

[…]

Adam Perlman, director of Duke's Integrative Medicine program, practices a similar type of medicine. "I don't just want to focus on getting people on the right medication," he says. "Just because you've gotten blood pressure in a normal range doesn't mean you've optimized someone's vitality. So I also like to focus on open-mindedness to things that fall outside mainstream medicine."

So Open-Minded Your Brain Falls Out

But in the long run, the Laidlers questioned—and eventually rejected—their initial open-mindedness. And today, despite the claims of added scientific rigor, many experts question the mindset of integrative practitioners like Katz and Perlman.

[...]

Reflecting on his experience, Jim Laidler concluded that false hope was like a drug. [...] After Disneyland, the Laidlers were able to apply similar thinking to their own situation. It turns out that withdrawal from false hope has a silver lining: it allows you to start looking for real hope.

As David continued to improve (without exotic treatments), Jim and Louise were forced to confront hard questions about their oldest son. Would Ben ever move out? Who would take care of him when they died? Over many years, they developed a plan. As a child, Jim had lived on a farm, and he remembered how there had always been something for everyone to do, no matter what their age or skill set. He and Louise set up a trust and an inheritance. Then they sought out families with autistic children about Ben's age, to see if they might be interested in joining together to start a group home.

"This planning—it was a better kind of happiness," Jim says. "I knew it was real. It was tangible." The Laidlers found three other families. They bought 17 acres of farmland. Together, the families found a couple to work as caretakers and built a home for their four boys, soon to be adults. At the end of this February, everything was ready. Ben and his three housemates moved into their own home.

"They grow peppers and herbs and sell them to local restaurants," Jim says proudly. "We hire college students in the area to take them on outings, to bowling, to watch football games, go out to dinner. And we're making sure it will keep working when we're gone."

None of that, he assures me, would ever have happened if he and Louise had continued to hope for an alternative cure. Although the previous regimen of supplements and dietary changes wasn't physically harmful, it still exacted a heavy toll in financial and mental resources. Had they continued to pursue it, Jim believes, there would have been no time, no money, and no willingness to think long-term. And eventually, their son would be an adult, and they wouldn't have known what to do. But now there is a plan, and they rest easier knowing that Ben will never have to live in a state-run home or move in with his brother. For the Laidlers, the real alternative was to stop believing in miracles—and start planning for the future.

EVALUATING THE AUTHOR'S ARGUMENTS:

Viewpoint author Alan Levinovitz shares the painful journey of one family and their experience with alternative medicine. Discuss a well-publicized topic from the media, such as the controversy of immunization, and compare it to the family story shared in this viewpoint.

There Is a Lack of Research Data on Alternative Medicine

Edzard Ernst

"Any therapy must be considered unsafe until the time we have sound data showing it is not unduly harmful."

In the following viewpoint, Edzard Ernst argues that it is difficult or maybe impossible to determine if alternative medical therapies are beneficial or not harmful. Ernst provides a brief summation of how the pharmaceuticals used in conventional medicine are tested both before and after being on the market for patients. He contrasts this with the almost total lack of reliable data available on the benefits and safety of alternative therapies. Ernst is a professor emeritus at the University of Exeter and was awarded the John Maddox Prize in 2015 for standing up for science.

AS YOU READ, CONSIDER THE FOLLOWING QUESTIONS:
1. What is efficacy as explained by the viewpoint article?
2. What is often missing in the evaluation of alternative medical therapy according to the author?
3. What challenge does Ernst issue to fans of alternative medical therapy?

"The harms of alternative medicine: what we see is just the tip of the iceberg," by Edzard Ernst, The Spectator (1828) Ltd, May 26, 2017. Reprinted by permission.

Many consider alternative medicine "snake oil," with little medicinal value.

M any people seem to think that the value of a therapy is determined by its efficacy: a treatment that is highly efficacious must be better than one that is less efficacious. Others seem to believe that it is the safety of a therapy which matters most: a treatment that causes no or few side effects must be good, one that has many is bad.

Such notions might appear logical, but they are mistaken. Things are usually more complicated. Some treatments can cause extremely serious side effects but are still extremely valuable. An example would be chemotherapy; it often causes all sorts of awful problems but, if it saves cancer patients' lives, it cannot be bad.

Other treatments might be virtually free of side effects, but they are nevertheless rubbish. Take crystal healing, for instance; it is hard to imagine that it causes any side effects but, as it also does not cure anything, it cannot possibly be a good therapy.

To determine the real value of a therapeutic intervention, we need to consider more than its efficacy alone and more than its safety alone. Obviously, we must look at the balance of the two factors.

When a new drug comes on the market, it has been tested thoroughly for efficacy; we therefore can be fairly sure that it works. But initially we know relatively little about its safety; in particular, we know little about possible rare side effects. Such knowledge requires data not just from the few hundred patients who took the drug when it was tested in efficacy trials, but we need data from a few hundred thousand patients.

To generate this information, drugs are monitored for side effects while they are used in routine practice. Should this "post-marketing surveillance" throw up any serious problems, the drug might be withdrawn from the market.

But this only applies to conventional medicine. In alternative medicine things are different, sometimes dramatically different. As the value of any therapy is determined by its risk/benefit balance, we would ideally want to know the efficacy and the safety of alternative

therapies too. Yet we often don't know enough about either.

Alternative therapies have not been tested for efficacy before they come on the market; they usually were in use long before we had the idea of licensing and regulating drugs. Consequently, we have little or only incomplete knowledge about their efficacy.

On the safety side of the equation, things are even worse. There is no post-marketing surveillance of alternative therapies, and all we know about their risks comes from the occasional case report published in the medical literature. This means that under-reporting of harms is huge, and our data are just the tip of the iceberg.

It follows that any attempt at evaluating a risk/benefit balance of alternative therapies is highly problematic. We usually know too little about both determinants to even begin a reasonable estimation. All we can do in this situation is rely on rough estimates.

If any given therapy generates no benefit because it is not efficacious, we can be sure that its risk/benefit quotient can never be positive. Dividing any finite number for risk, however small, by zero gives an infinitely large figure. We can furthermore assume that, for any therapy that is only marginally efficacious and thus generates only a small benefit, even a very small risk would result in an unfavourable risk/benefit balance.

Finally, we can say that an alternative therapy that is known to cause serious harm, the benefit would need to be substantial for its risk/benefit balance to come out favourable.

And what about those alternative therapies for which we have not enough information to attempt even such rudimentary analyses?

Alternative practitioners and their followers tend to think that we must give them the benefit of the doubt. This is a dangerously misguided view.

In the interest of our patients, we ought to consider any intervention to be inefficacious until we have good evidence to the contrary. Similarly, any therapy must be considered unsafe until the time we have sound data showing it is not unduly harmful. Giving alternative therapies the benefit of the doubt is therefore not an option.

Such talk is alarmist, claim fans of alternative medicine. After debating with them ad nauseam, I now have this challenge for them: show me your list of alternative therapies that demonstrably are associated with a favourable risk/benefit balance. Considering that there are more than 400 different alternative therapies and that most of them are used for a wide range of conditions, such a list could potentially be very long indeed.

But I will be modest: if you can list more than a dozen alternative therapies for specific conditions, I promise to never write about the risk/benefit balance of alternative medicine again.

EVALUATING THE AUTHOR'S ARGUMENTS:

Viewpoint author Edzard Ernst maintains that alternative medicine practitioners and their followers think that their treatments must be given the benefit of the doubt. What does this mean? Do you agree, and why do you think this is?

Viewpoint 5

We Must Consider New Ideas to Treat Diseases

Scott Daniels

"Just because a treatment is not practiced by the mainstream does not mean it is ineffective. It is just not accepted."

In the following viewpoint, Scott Daniels argues that current treatments for cancer are ineffective and that by delegitimizing alternative therapies, doctors and patients are missing out on cures. The author uses the framework of countering responses to a previous article he'd written to further explain his point. Although the author is not a medical professional and lacks enough scientific knowledge to emit authority, he makes the case that conventional medicine does not have all the answers. Daniels created the website Provide Your Own, which features his thoughts on a variety of topics.

AS YOU READ, CONSIDER THE FOLLOWING QUESTIONS:
1. Does the author believe chemotherapy is an effective treatment for cancer?
2. What is sugar's relationship to cancer, as proposed by the author?
3. What does the author mean when he says vitamin D3 is not considered a miracle drug because it is not a patented drug?

The chaga mushroom has been found to kill cancer cells and stimulate the immune system in animals.

My article "The Cancer Fraud" has begun to elicit criticism from defenders of conventional medicine. It is difficult to change paradigms, especially when so much is at stake. My heart goes out to cancer sufferers and their families. However difficult it is to consider new ideas, we must face them if we are to avoid the inevitable suffering that cancer produces. Conventional medicine is an abysmal failure in treating cancer. It is time to face that fact.

A defender of conventional medicine has raised some good points that I would like to address. Following are his points and my response to each one.

Effectiveness of Conventional Treatments

> *"You know what you call alternative medicine that works? Medicine. Until that point alternative medicine has either been proven to be not right, or not proven to be right."*

Your definition of conventional medicine is treatments that have proven effective, while alternative medicine is comprised of treatments that are not proven in their effectiveness. When they are, they become conventional medicine.

While in an ideal world, this idea would be sound. In an ideal world, men would always tell the truth. Men would not hide, distort, or even overlook information for personal gain. In an ideal world, doctors would be able to sift through the latest research without pressures or preconceived ideas. In an ideal world, we all could shift our paradigms the moment the current one appears to be false. Unfortunately, we do not live in an ideal world.

The world we live in is full of fraud, greed, cherished paradigms, and just plain ignorance. In this world, valid treatments do exist for cancer, and they are either unknown by mainstream practitioners or rejected for various reasons. I cover that in my article. Just because a treatment is not practiced by the mainstream does not mean it is ineffective. It is just not accepted. I'll cover the effectiveness of alternative treatments in the next section. In this section, I will cover the effectiveness of conventional treatments.

A chart listing various five-year survival rates for different types of cancers when treated by chemotherapy shows a survival rate of a whopping 2.1 percent. A review of chemo on five-year survival rates in Australia garnered almost identical results, with a 2.3 percent success rate.

I would hardly call chemotherapy a treatment that works. In my personal experience, I have never known or heard of anyone who has survived the five-year mark. These studies bear out my personal experience – only 2 people out of 100 live more than five years when treated with chemotherapy.

Conventional medicine has always been fraught with problems, and will always be. For years, doctors mocked the idea of hand washing, and more recently, the doctor who discovered the bacterial source of ulcers was ridiculed until the evidence was too overwhelming to ignore.

That is not to say that alternative medicine doesn't suffer as well. Both approaches suffer from the same problems. Both are practiced by men. Imperfect men. Effective treatments must be found where they exist. The imprimatur granted to conventional medicine is no guarantee of success as these five-year cancer studies show.

Effectiveness of Alternative Treatments

"You had me right up to the point of reading this gem: "It is the lies, cover-up, and outright persecution of anyone who

tells the truth about cancer being a dietary disease that can be effectively reversed without medical treatment.' Seriously – a dietary disease? Reversed without medical treatment?? Where's your proof? Where are your clinical trials? How many people have YOU saved?"

Many people have been effectively cured of cancer via alternative treatments. While I am not a practitioner, there are many who are successfully treating cancer. Many of these people are actual MDs. Unfortunately they are hard to find. If their practice is especially effective, they are often shut down.

As far as clinical studies of actual treatments, how can there ever be any, when anyone who has a promising treatment is shut down? There are numerous studies showing the efficacy of dietary factors on cancer as I'll discuss next. These are mainstream studies. Nevertheless, they are ignored. Completely ignored.

To my naysayers, I say: "You can call these alternative cancer practitioners snake oil salesmen if you want, but ask yourself this question: what will it take to convince you? When your local oncologist embraces alternative treatments? The biggest resistors to change throughout history have been doctors and scientists. They have vested interests in the status quo, and they are not about to embrace changes. That is the sad fact. It is time to face it."

Cancer and Its Relationship to Diet

"My mother was SAVED by medical intervention for her cancer. Without it she would be DEAD. I've also had to bury relatives who DIED because of cancer. And it had nothing to do with their diet."

The assertion that their diet was irrelevant is a bold one, and I insist on the same level of proof of its verity that this reader demands from me. He asserts these cancers had nothing to do with their diet. I can understand his anger. Let's just assume for the moment that cancer is indeed caused by our diet. What then? It means that we are in some measure responsible. Our ignorance, our lack of self-control, our unwillingness to have an open mind contributed to these awful outcomes. How can we live with ourselves if we faced the truth? To lose a loved one is horrible, just horrible. We can bear it only if we believe that we did the "best we could." And I am not saying these individuals did otherwise. But, if they suffered due to ignorance, then does it justify remaining ignorant?

What about when the next loved one gets cancer? And the next? What will it take to open people's minds?

I have these questions for this writer about these cancer victims' diets: "Did they eat sugar, corn syrup, or any carbohydrates other than those found in green vegetables and fruits in their whole state? Did they eliminate all sources of vegetable oils from their diet? Did they take large amounts of fish oil daily? Did they take massive amounts of vitamin D3?"

Unless they had all of these diet practices, no one can say it had nothing to do with their diet. Not only that, these are merely the biggest and most obvious items. Let's look at each one in more detail:

Sugar and Starches

It is a well-known fact that cancer feeds on sugar. Even mainstream medicine acknowledges this fact. Do oncologists tell their patients to avoid these sources of excess sugar? No. Not convinced? One article cites a study using a mouse model that showed a direct correlation to the survival rate of breast cancer to blood sugar levels. Want something more mainstream? How about an article from Reuters that states: "Tumor cells thrive on sugar but they used the fructose to proliferate."

With the abundant evidence for removing sugar and starches from the diet, how can anyone say that diet has no relationship to cancer?

Omega-3 Fatty Acids

Numerous studies show the relationship of excess omega-6 fatty acids as compared to omega-3 fatty acids. Dr. Mercola has even cited an instance of a man curing himself of cancer by taking large doses of fish oil.

Vitamin D3

If vitamin D3 were a patented drug, it would be hailed as the miracle drug of the twenty-first century. It is not, so its profound benefits for are largely ignored. It would take several articles to chronicle all its benefits. Here is a juicy one for you – taking vitamin D slashes the risk of breast cancer by 50 percent. Vitamin D is cited as having a key role in preventing the development of cancer. Another source lists over 800 clinical studies citing the positive effects of vitamin D on cancer.

Conclusion

This reader wanted evidence for alternative treatments. In addition to the numerous practitioners – both M.D.s and non-M.D.s who are successfully treating thousands of patients, there are thousands of studies showing the benefits in both preventing and treating cancers with various diet factors and supplements. I have cited just a handful. If one really wants more proof, one only has to search the internet for these studies. Despite the plethora of evidence, the vanguards of cancer research such as the National Cancer Institute continue to say the results are inconclusive. In the instance I linked to, they cite studies that use inadequate levels of vitamin D, and then say the results are inconclusive.

It is not for lack of evidence that effective cancer treatments are not widely adopted. It is rather the unwillingness of so many to accept the evidence.

The sad fact is: men must preserve the status quo when it is in their interests. It doesn't matter how many people suffer and die as a result.

EVALUATING THE AUTHOR'S ARGUMENTS:

Viewpoint author Scott Daniels asserts many strong opinions without professional scientific or medical credentials. While he does cite several articles to support his opinions, they also could be considered anecdotal. Do you think the author successfully defended his points to those who responded to his original article? Why or why not?

Alternative Cancer Remedies May Result in Early Death

"It seems sound to assume that Mr. Jobs's choice for alternative medicine has eventually led to an unnecessarily early death."

Sandra Ryan

In the following viewpoint, Sandra Ryan argues that pursuing alternative remedies to treat cancer wastes precious time, which can have fatal results. Ryan presents many facts from doctors who have witnessed patients dying unnecessarily early and cites Apple CEO Steve Jobs's cancer treatment as a perfect example—Jobs put off conventional treatment until it was too late, and according to some doctors, most likely died prematurely because of his decision. Sandra Ryan is a medical journalist and editor at the *Irish Medical News*.

AS YOU READ, CONSIDER THE FOLLOWING QUESTIONS:
1. What is the difference between complementary and alternative therapies?
2. How is the Irish Cancer Society an opponent of alternative cancer remedies?
3. Identify two reasons why cancer patients undergo alternative therapy.

Echinachea for colds, ginkgo biloba for memory, and glucosamine for arthritis are just some of the herbal remedies taken by millions of people around the world. But they all have something else in common: none of them have been proven to be effective.

In clinical trials funded by the National Center for Complementary and Alternative Medicine in the United States, which spent $2.5 billion of taxpayers' money over ten years trying to find out whether certain alternative remedies actually work, the only one with clear evidence of effectiveness was ginger, which was found to be helpful in relieving nausea in patients taking chemotherapy for cancer.

The use of alternative therapies to treat cancer is controversial. Despite absolutely no evidence supporting their use, millions of people still take them. Figures for Ireland are not available, but the market in the UK is worth around £210 million, reports show, with one-in-five adults thought to be consumers. Research has also estimated that up to 60 percent of cancer patients try unconventional remedies and about 40 percent take vitamin or dietary supplements.

When it was revealed that the late Steve Jobs deliberately delayed his recommended treatment for pancreatic cancer in order to take alternative medicines, the debate over their use and effectiveness was heightened. Shortly after Jobs's death, one cancer specialist from Harvard University, Ramzi Amri, wrote: "Mr. Jobs allegedly chose to undergo all sorts of alternative treatment options before opting for conventional medicine…given the circumstances, it seems sound to assume that Mr. Jobs's choice for alternative medicine has eventually led to an unnecessarily early death."

It should be pointed out that there is a difference between alternative therapies and complementary therapies. The latter refers to treatments that are used along with standard or mainstream medical treatment. Examples may include meditation to reduce stress or peppermint or ginger tea for nausea.

Alternative medicine, however, is used instead of mainstream, recommended treatment. Alternative therapies are either unproven because they have not been scientifically tested, or they have been disproved (studied and found not to work).

The Irish Cancer Society says it does not recommend the use of alternative therapies in place of conventional treatments for cancer.

The late Steve Jobs has been cited as an example of the danger of prolonging cancer treatment in the pursuit of alternative therapies.

A spokesperson said:

> *There is often little or no medical or scientific evidence to prove the claims of unlicensed practitioners who maintain to have the "cure" for cancer. We recommend the use of conventional therapies under the supervision of licensed medical practitioners for the treatment of cancer. Conventional therapies include surgery, radiotherapy, chemotherapy, hormonal and biological therapies.*

According to an article in a 2008 edition of *Fortune* magazine, for nine months between 2003 and 2004 Steve Jobs (a vegetarian) chose "alternative methods to treat his pancreatic cancer, hoping to avoid [an] operation through a special diet."

Then in July 2004 he had surgery because his cancer had spread throughout his liver.

The suggestion from Dr. Amri and other cancer specialists who commented on his case (but did not treat Mr. Jobs) is that he wasted precious time trying alternative therapies.

Along with the Irish Cancer Society, neither professional medical oncologists nor alternative medicine organizations recommend that patients forgo proven medical therapy to go down an alternative route. So why do patients do it?

The Placebo Effect: "It Makes Me Feel Better"

For every person who says that homeopathy (a disproven alternative therapy that claims a disease can be cured by a substance that produces similar symptoms in healthy people), for example, has cured their illness, there are 99 people (probably more) who have seen no benefits – except perhaps psychological ones.

The placebo effect is a well-documented physiological and psychological phenomenon whereby a person's symptoms disappear when no effective treatment has been taken (a placebo, or "sugar pill," is used in clinical trials to test the efficacy of a drug). Some studies have shown that even after a patient is told they are taking a placebo, it continues to be effective.

Even proponents of herbal medicines acknowledge the placebo effect. Last year Professor Edzard Ernst, professor of complementary medicine at the Peninsula Medical School in the UK, stepped down from the role after 18 years, many of which were spent doing research. According to Professor Ernst, 95 percent of the treatments he examined are "statistically indistinguishable" from placebo treatments. There was only a clear benefit above and beyond a placebo in 5 percent of cases (which included the depression remedy St. John's Wort).

But tell this to someone determined a particular alternative therapy will or does work and you will probably get nowhere. Some cancer patients would perhaps understandably rather take something known for its purported healing and soothing properties than something that causes them to get sick and lose their hair.

How Does Conventional Cancer Treatment Work?

People with cancer now have access to more effective therapies than ever before, and Irish patients are in a unique position with regard to these treatments; in Ireland, at least for the time being, oncologists are not restricted by the HSE and can prescribe cancer drugs as needed and when necessary – one of the only countries in the Western world where this is the case (although this may soon change with ongoing plans by the Health Minister and HSE to save money on drug spending).

Two of the most effective (and expensive) cancer drugs are Avastin and Herceptin, which directly target cancerous cells, as opposed to chemotherapy, which attacks every and any cell that divides in the body, hoping to damage the rapidly dividing cancerous ones. These drugs and others like them changed cancer treatment by changing the way doctors target the disease in their patients.

Other groundbreaking drugs, called tyrosine-kinase inhibitors (such as Tarceva or Iressa, used in lung cancer), target gene mutations that are now known to be linked to cancerous growth in certain patients. The discovery of such gene mutations has led scientists to hope that eventually, and where possible, these mutations will be discovered before they have a chance to cause cancer. The decades of rigorous testing and research that led to such developments do not exist in the world of alternative medicine.

One oncologist who works in a large Dublin teaching hospital and who wished not to be named, in order to protect the anonymity of his cancer patients, is highly critical of alternative and complementary therapies. The oncologist said:

> I have seen cancer patients literally waste months of what little life they have left researching herbal treatments, or taking them, or arguing with their family and loved ones about taking them. There are websites and sham specialists in Ireland and abroad who promise cures and tumour shrinkage and it's understandable that, faced with death, some people cling to this and hope, of course it is.

He continued: "Many patients, especially in pancreatic cancer or oesophageal cancer, present to us so late that they have even less time. The earlier cancer is detected and the earlier treatment begins, the better the chance. Patients can buy anything online and you don't even know what is in these compounds. I had one patient say he wasn't going to "poison his body" with chemo anymore because it made him sicker and wasn't working. He was reading these websites that say cancer treatment is a scheme cooked up by rich companies and doctors; one of those crazy sites that say the moon landing was faked, that sort of thing. This patient was dead in less than a year. We have to stress to patients that cancer treatment is tough and sometimes the best you'll get is an extra two months of life...but in medicine you treat with what has been proven to work.

"All it takes is one or two patients who have been taking some kind of alternative medicine and whose cancer entered remission or didn't progress, and they are held up as proof they can work. Which is dangerous. You can have the flu and eat an apple every day; if the flu doesn't turn into pneumonia you don't thank the apples."

As pointed out by this oncologist, a general suspicion of "Big Pharma" can also be the problem. However, a drug is not licensed for use just because a pharmaceutical company spends millions marketing it. Much like the world of law, a drug is assumed to be ineffective until proven to be useful. Doctors only focus on drugs that have spent years going through carefully controlled and monitored clinical studies – they do not prescribe a drug simply because a drug company says it works.

Doctors want to cure cancer and help their patients, probably at any cost. The accepted, conventional cancer drugs are expensive and, as explained above, can be toxic. If specialists believed herbal medicines could cure or diminish someone's cancer they would be recommending it, and it would be standard therapy. Anyone who holds the view that "poisoning your body" with cancer treatment is not the way to beat the disease should think carefully, and perhaps learn something from Steve Jobs's case, before ignoring specialist advice. Cancer patients don't have time to waste.

EVALUATING THE AUTHOR'S ARGUMENTS:

In this viewpoint Sandra Ryan discusses the dangers of alternative therapies for cancer treatment. Using specific evidence from the viewpoint explain how conspiracy theories, suspicion of "Big Pharma" and placebos conflict with conventional cancer treatment.

Chapter 3

How Should the Practice of Alternative Medicine Be Changed?

Is there room for both scientifically backed medicine and alternative therapies?

CAM Therapies Must Undergo Rigorous Scientific Research and Testing

"Like all other areas of health care practice and consumption, complementary therapies need to be underwritten by rigorous scientific investigation."

Jon Adams

In the following viewpoint, Jon Adams maintains that for the good of public health, research and scientific testing of alternative therapies should and must be carried out. Adams reports that complementary and alternative medicine is big business in Australia like elsewhere around the world, and that Australia is already carrying out this research. Adams is a professor of public health, and director of the Australian Research Center in Sydney, Australia.

AS YOU READ, CONSIDER THE FOLLOWING QUESTIONS:
1. According to Adams what type of testing should alternative therapies be subjected to?
2. Which country has already embarked on alternative therapy research as reported by Adams?
3. As stated by the viewpoint, what two beliefs have possibly interfered with research and testing of alternative therapies?

"Here's why we should research alternative therapies", by Jon Adams, The Conversation, February 12, 2014. https://theconversation.com/heres-why-we-should-research-alternative-therapies-19436. Licensed under CC BY-ND 4.0 International.

Rigorous scientific research and testing might help certain CAM therapies gain acceptance.

Acupuncture, chiropractic, herbal medicines, massage, and other therapies known collectively as complementary and alternative medicine, are big business in Australia, as elsewhere.

About two thirds of Australians use such products and practices over the course of a year. Nonetheless, the debate around these therapies remains dominated by emotive and political commentary – on both sides.

Doing the Right Kind of Research

Like all other areas of health care practice and consumption, complementary therapies need to be underwritten by rigorous scientific investigation. The gold standard of such work is the randomized controlled trial, which aims to establish whether a treatment or medicine is clinically efficacious.

This type of research is to be applauded and encouraged. But the current popularity of alternative therapies highlights the immediate need for parallel public health and health-services research.

What we need is a broad range and mix of methods and approaches that are essential to understanding the place and use of complementary therapies within contemporary health care.

Such an approach provides findings of direct benefit to practice and policy. It would be in the interest of patients, practitioners, and those managing and directing health policy to address critical questions such as why, when, and how alternative therapies are currently consumed and practiced.

Studies along these lines help provide a factual platform for ensuring safe, effective health care. And it's important to note that such investigations are neither for complementary medicine nor against it.

Rather, the work is undertaken in the spirit of critical and rigorous empirical study that charts a path free from the emotion we have become accustomed to on this topic.

A Burgeoning Body of Work

A number of recent Australian projects have started to do just this kind of research, to explore the use and practice of alternative therapies from a critical public health and health-services research perspective.

Research drawing on a large, nationally representative sample of 1,835 pregnant women, for instance, has shown that complementary therapies are popular for pregnancy-related conditions. The researchers found nearly half (49.4 percent) of the women they studied had consulted an alternative-therapy practitioner at the same time as a maternity-care provider for a pregnancy-related condition.

Similarly, another study found 40 percent of Australian women with back pain who were surveyed had consulted a complementary -therapy practitioner, as well as a health provider for back pain.

Other Australian research has found that women in rural areas are statistically more likely to use alternative medicine than their counterparts in urban Australia.

And use has been identified as high among older Australian men and women as well as among people with depression, cancer, and a range of chronic conditions.

In these and other areas of health-seeking behaviour and utilization, the core issues requiring further examination include how people make the decision to use complementary therapies, and how they seek information and engage with them.

Uncovering Use

The use of alternative therapies is often a hidden activity within the community and, in many cases, distanced from both formal care and health care providers (and, in some cases, divorced from complementary therapists as well). This raises a number of potential risks around safety, efficiency, and coordination of care.

While many people condemn complementary and alternative therapies because of a lack of clinical evidence, this doesn't constitute a scientific platform for ignoring or denying research on the subject.

In fact, it's the opposite case. If we accept that most complementary therapies have at best emerging, weak, or no clinical evidence, then it surely becomes necessary to try and more fully understand what drives people to use them, in what manner and setting they use them, and what information they draw upon to decide whether they'll use them.

At a time when health care funding is stretched by our aging population and rise of chronic illnesses, it's imperative that research-based assessments of future practice, policy, and financial planning include consideration of all health treatments.

Such research will not only help produce a critical, non-partisan platform for better understanding complementary and alternative therapies, it will also provide a rigorous and broad evidence base with which to help people, practitioners, and policymakers on this significant component of Australians' health care.

EVALUATING THE AUTHOR'S ARGUMENTS:

In this viewpoint Jon Adams maintains that complementary and alternative treatments should be subjected to rigorous scientific testing. Since so many people are using alternative therapies it simply makes sense to determine the true benefits if any of these treatments so health practitioners could recommend what actually works. Which doctors, or researchers, from previous viewpoints would agree with this? Cite specific examples to back up your ideas.

Industry Must Supply Funding for CAM Research

"There are limited government funding options for complementary medicine research so it's important that industry supports such research."

Andrew Scholey

In the following viewpoint, Andrew Scholey maintains that research into complementary medicine should be funded by industry if government options are not available. Scholey uses case in point studies of Australian research to back his thesis, and contends that the same rigorous scientific safety and efficacy studies should be carried on whether done by government institutions or industry. Scholey is professor and director of the Centre for Human Psychopharmacology at Swinburne University of Technology in Australia.

AS YOU READ, CONSIDER THE FOLLOWING QUESTIONS:

1. How is industry funded research the same as government funded research according to Scholey?
2. As reported by Scholey, how is research and research data monitored?
3. According to the viewpoint, how is research rigor maintained?

If alternative therapies can potentially help then research funding should be made available.

There's been a fair bit of debate recently over the role of industry funding in research into complementary and alternative medicines, including on this site. Much of it has argued that research funded by industry is inherently compromised, but it doesn't have to be.

There are limited government funding options in Australia for complementary medicine research so it's important that industry supports such research. It's equally important that there are mechanisms in place to ensure the research is conducted at a high level, with checks on quality, such as trial registration and peer review of papers.

Show Me the Money

In Australia, there are two major government bodies that fund research—the National Health and Medical Research Council (NHMRC) and the Australian Research Council (ARC). Since 2012, the ARC no longer funds health or medical research at all, while the NHMRC largely restricts its funding of clinical trials to those investigating medical and health conditions. If we wish to find out whether or not a dietary supplement improves some aspect of health among people without a defined medical condition, the choice is effectively between industry-supported research or no research.

Indeed, in my experience, it's not unheard of to receive feedback for grant applications saying although the science is sound, the research should be supported by industry! This suggests that there is a reasonably common belief that such support, when available, is more appropriate for these kinds of studies.

Even if this position changed, competition for research support is so high that, last year, for instance, the NHMRC funded around 16 percent of applications for its highly regarded project grants. So it's likely industry will play an increasingly valuable role in supporting Australian research.

But researchers don't just undertake industry-funded research because of the lack of other funding. The motivation for scientific investigation is the same for any academic – to increase our understanding and knowledge.

Ensuring Research Integrity

Industry-funded research is subject to the same peer-review processes as any other. Peer reviewers are made aware of funding sources and judge research on its merit. If it's of a high enough quality, the research is published in well-regarded international journals.

The gold standard for testing the efficacy of any health intervention is the clinical trial—a controlled study involving human volunteers. Like studies of pharmaceutical drugs, research into the health effects of nutritional supplements relies on clinical trials.

The requirements for research to support health claims from nutritional interventions and supplements have varying levels of stringency in the United States, Europe, and Australia, but all trials should be conducted to the standards of good clinical practice.

This involves registering the study on a public clinical trials registry, such as the Australian New Zealand Clinical Trials Registry, to ensure the research is transparent.

Industry-sponsored trials also routinely use statisticians not associated with the researchers, who follow a predetermined statistical plan.

Typically, studies are monitored by independent auditors to ensure all data are recorded and entered into the database accurately. This database is "locked" prior to analysis, which is performed using codes so the statistician cannot tell the active treatment data set from the placebo data set.

These processes are time consuming, resource-heavy and not always pleasant but most scientists welcome the rigor they add to their work. Interestingly, most studies funded by national grant funding schemes are not subject to the same level of scrutiny.

Growing Sophistication

It is difficult to know whether researchers unconsciously put a positive spin on industry-sponsored studies by exaggerating certain outcomes to ensure continued funding. But is there any reason to think the reporting of research funded by other sources cannot also be (unconsciously) spun to avoid being among the 84 percent of applicants who don't get funding the next time around?

In order to maintain rigor, researchers working with alternative medicines have an obligation to report negative or null (when the intervention does harm or does nothing) findings. In my experience, this is always written into the research contract.

Of course, statements made for the purposes of marketing can be appallingly misleading. But this is completely independent of the science undertaken to evaluate the efficacy of products, and could be avoided by consultation with the researchers involved.

The funding landscape in Australia is becoming increasingly sophisticated and, as with other areas, industry support for alternative medicines has its place.

EVALUATING THE AUTHOR'S ARGUMENTS:

Viewpoint author Andrew Scholey writes, "statements made for the purposes of marketing can be appallingly misleading." How might marketing impact reports of testing data or results?

Stop Wasting Time and Money on Clinical Testing of Alternative Treatments

"Such research only serves to lend legitimacy to otherwise dubious practices."

Daily Mail

In the following viewpoint, the *Daily Mail* features two critics who argue that time and money should not be wasted on experimental testing of alternative therapies that have already been proven to be ineffective. Testimony by scientists condemns the continued testing of homeopathy, Reiki, and aromatherapy because in their view these practices could never be considered anything but pseudoscience. Instead, these experts argue that doctors should be able to take time to understand the medical conditions of their patients and prescribe appropriate science-based medical treatment rather than on ineffective alternative treatments. The *Daily Mail* is a British daily newspaper.

"Clinical trials of 'quack alternative medicines should be stopped because they are damaging and a waste of money', say two leading critics," MailOnline, August 20, 2014. Reprinted by permission.

AS YOU READ, CONSIDER THE FOLLOWING QUESTIONS:
1. What treatments are considered pseudoscientific in the viewpoint?
2. Why is research into pseudoscientific treatments unfortunate according to the viewpoint?
3. According to the Reiki Council spokeswoman quoted, what does Reiki therapy help with?

Clinical trials of "quack" alternative medicines should be stopped because they are damaging and financially wasteful, two leading critics have said.

US scientists David Gorski, a professor of surgery and oncology at Wayne State University, and Steven Novella, an assistant professor in neurology at Yale School of Medicine, launched a scathing attack of treatments including aromatherapy, homeopathy, and Reiki.

They condemned scientists who continue to carry out controlled experiments to discover whether the "highly implausible treatments" work.

The pair brand homeopathy and Reiki as "faith healing," claiming clinical trials of the treatments have "already been proved to have no benefits whatsoever," and "merely lend them legitimacy and take money away from more deserving projects."

The article came just weeks after Conservative MP David Tredinnick praised the fact herbal remedies and healing were now becoming accepted in parts of the NHS, and called for astrology to be incorporated into the health service.

Professor Gorski said: "We hope this will be the first of many opportunities to discuss in the peer-reviewed literature the perils and pitfalls of doing clinical trials on treatment modalities that have already been refuted by basic science.

"The two key examples in the article, homeopathy and Reiki, are about as close to impossible from basic science considerations alone as you can imagine. Homeopathy involves diluting substances away to nothing and beyond, while Reiki is in essence faith healing that substitutes Eastern mysticism for Christian beliefs, as can be

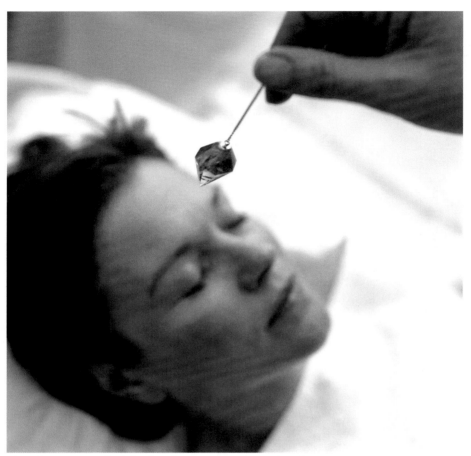

Should precious medical funding be spent on studying the effectiveness of crystal therapy treatment?

demonstrated by substituting the word 'god' for the 'universal source' that Reiki masters claim to be able to tap into to channel their 'healing energy' into patients."

Professor Novella argued clinical trials of such treatments would not change the minds of those who already practice them but might make people who are tempted to try them believe they might actually work. He said: "Studying highly implausible treatments is a losing proposition. Such studies are unlikely to demonstrate benefit, and proponents are unlikely to stop using the treatment when the study is negative. Such research only serves to lend legitimacy to otherwise dubious practices."

The professors, who run a blog about integrating science and medicine, have called for changes in the medical system to ensure doctors have the time to truly treat patients "holistically" by listening to them and taking account of their circumstances before prescribing them medicine.

They argue this course will bring far more success than doctors offering patients treatments that claim to heal the body and mind but really have no success.

Professor Gorski added: "Somehow this idea has sprung up that to be a 'holistic' doctor you have to embrace pseudoscience like homeopathy, Reiki, traditional Chinese medicine, and the like, but that's a false dichotomy. If the medical system is currently too impersonal and patients are rushed through office visits because a doctor has to see more and more patients to cover his salary and expenses, then the answer is to find a way to fix those problems, not to embrace quackery. Integrating pseudoscience with science-based medicine isn't going to make science-based medicine better.

"One of our bloggers, Mark Crislip, has a fantastic saying for this: 'If you mix cow pie with apple pie, it does not make the cow pie taste better; it makes the apple pie worse.' With CAM or 'integrative medicine,' that's exactly what we're doing, and these clinical trials of magic are just more examples of it."

Professors Gorski and Novella have also called on patients to use their own common sense when looking at the evidence to decide for themselves whether a treatment actually works or not.

Professor Gorski added: "Critical thinking will help patients learn to recognize when a course of treatment is not supported by data or to tell when a health claim from any practitioner is just too good to be true."

The article was published in the journal *Trends in Molecular Medicine*. A spokeswoman for the Reiki Council said: "There is a growing grassroots demand for therapies such as Reiki as people report significant improvements in their well-being. This is backed up by a research database that, despite the lack of funding, is beginning to suggest benefits particularly in the arena of stress, depression and anxiety. Increasing numbers of hospitals and hospice offer Reiki for their patients—a snowballing effect due to patient demand and medical professionals observations."

EVALUATING THE AUTHOR'S ARGUMENTS:

In this viewpoint, the Daily Mail quotes several experts that are opponents to clinical testing of certain alternative therapies. Explain in your own words what the "cow pie, apple pie" metaphor means with respect to science-based medicine and pseudoscience.

Anti-Science Sentiments Have Encouraged the Rise of Alternative Medicine

"The anti-scientific sentiments behind alternative medicine are disturbingly widespread in the United States."

Joel Gottsegen

In the following viewpoint, Joel Gottsegen exposes what appears to be a fraudulent method by a well-known alternative medicine practitioner. Gottsegen maintains that by the false use of scientific sounding language the general public is being misled into believing that alternative medicine has healing properties, which may actually be a placebo effect. Gottsegen argues that the anti-science attitude and reluctance to submit alternative treatments to rigorous scientific testing clouds the entire issue, which then causes a large mistrust of other overwhelming scientifically proven issues. Gottsegen wrote for the *Standford Daily* newspaper as a computer studies major at Stanford University.

"Alternative medicine is not medicine," by Joel Gottsegen, The Stanford Daily, October 30, 2014. Reprinted by permission.

AS YOU READ, CONSIDER THE FOLLOWING QUESTIONS:
1. According to Gottsegen, how does Deepak Chopra appear to fool the public?
2. What is the biggest problem of alternative medicine practitioners according to the author?
3. How does alternative medicine hurt basic science and scientific awareness as stated by the viewpoint?

D eepak Chopra is living large. With an estimated net worth of $80 million, the New Age author could be forgiven for being a bit defensive about his affluence. In a 2012 interview, he declared: "Spiritual people should not be ashamed of being wealthy."

Chopra should not be put on trial for simply having a fortune. Whether he should be taken to task for how he made that fortune, however, is an entirely different question. Chopra is a leader of the so-called holistic medicine movement, a type of healing that claims to treat the whole person, rather than just the disease. In practice, this type of medicine often involves treatments and methods that the mainstream medical community disavows, like homeopathy and Ayurvedic medicine.

It is fair to say that Chopra lives within this scientific fringe. His medical theories are drawn from a strange mix of Eastern philosophy and contemporary science, the buzzwords of which he has been known to appropriate and apply completely out of context. In his book *Quantum Healing*, Chopra claims that because quantum entanglement links everything in the universe, it must be responsible for creating consciousness. He also introduced the concept of quantum healing, which he defines as the ability of one mode of consciousness to spontaneously correct the mistakes in another mode of consciousness. Chopra refers to such a correction — physicists, prepare to wince — as a quantum leap.

When questioned on his misuse of scientific terminology by Richard Dawkins, the famous skeptic, Chopra said that he had been using the term quantum as a metaphor, and that his definition of the word had little to do with its origins in quantum physics. This begs the question: If the concept that Chopra is trying to communicate has little

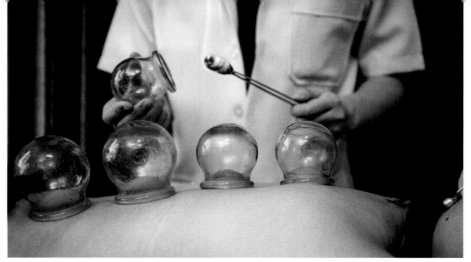

Is the ancient alternative treatment cupping scientifically legitimate?

to do with quantum physics, why would he use terms like "quantum entanglement"? While it is possible that Chopra really was attempting a poorly conceived metaphor, it seems more likely that he is using scientific jargon to add an aura of respectability to his fringe theories.

The bizarre medical theories expounded by Chopra and his colleagues might be complete nonsense, but it would be going too far to say that they do not help anyone. There are many people who claim that alternative medicine healed them after traditional methods failed. However, it is important to note that many of the success stories of alternative medicine involve illnesses that center on the subjective experience of the patient, like depression and chronic pain. These types of illness are much more likely to be alleviated using the placebo effect than medical issues like cancer and paralysis. Given this, it is unsurprising that an article in the *Atlantic* heralding "The Triumph of New Age Medicine" focuses on a retired firefighter with back pain, rather than someone with late-stage AIDS.

Helping people with chronic pain via the placebo effect is nice, but there are many ways to achieve this effect that create less collateral damage. Giving someone a sugar pill is relatively simple. Creating an enormous ideological framework that clouds people's judgements about mainstream medicine is not. The biggest problem with practitioners of alternative medicine is that they often deny the soundness of scientific studies as a measurement of the efficacy of a treatment. This is a dangerous sentiment. If Deepak Chopra were to discover a new form of medical treatment that helped sick people, it should be possible to test that the treatment is actually working. By denying the validity of the scientific method, alternative healers free themselves from any kind of accountability.

The anti-scientific sentiments behind alternative medicine are disturbingly widespread in the United States. They are the reason that one in four Americans is skeptical about global warming, despite overwhelming consensus within the scientific community. They are the reason that one in three parents believes that vaccines can cause autism, again despite overwhelming scientific consensus. These are bad numbers. They are damaging to the health of children and to the health of the planet. And they are made possible by the belief, furthered by proponents of alternative medicine, that the scientific method is inadequate.

Do not indulge Deepak Chopra. Even though a bit of quantum healing might seem benign, it contributes to an atmosphere that stifles rational thought.

I leave you with a quote from Tim Minchin, whose fantastic short film *Storm* does a fantastic job of dismantling the fuzzy logic behind the holistic medicine movement: "You know what they call alternative medicine that's been proved to work? Medicine."

EVALUATING THE AUTHOR'S ARGUMENTS:

In this viewpoint Joel Gottsegen contends that a big problem surrounding alternative healers is that they shun responsibility of authentic experimental testing, thereby freeing "themselves from any kind of accountability." Do you agree or disagree with this statement? Explain.

The Only Treatments That Beat Cancer Are Conventional

"People who chose alternative medicine instead of conventional cancer treatments were much less likely to survive for at least five years."

National Library of Medicine

In the following viewpoint, the National Library of Medicine analyzes a study published in a peer-reviewed medical journal that compares five-year survival rates for cancer patients. The NLM cites statistics that compare the types of medical treatment used, namely conventional versus alternative, and also the type of cancer treated. The study concludes that conventional treatment provides the best survival rate. The National Library of Medicine is the world's largest medical library.

AS YOU READ, CONSIDER THE FOLLOWING QUESTIONS:
1. According to the viewpoint, what are four conventional treatments for cancer?
2. What distinction is made between alternative and complementary treatments according to the author?
3. What does this study conclude as reported in the viewpoint?

"'Alternative cancer therapies' may increase your risk of death," National Library of Medicine (NLM), August 16, 2017.

Studies thus far have not proven any effectiveness of alternative treatments, such as certain medicinal plants, on cancer.

"Cancer patients who use alternative medicine more than twice as likely to die," is the stark message from *The Independent*. Researchers found that people who chose alternative medicine instead of conventional cancer treatments were much less likely to survive for at least five years.

Conventional treatments include surgery, radiotherapy, chemotherapy, or hormone treatments. The research only applies to people who choose not to have conventional treatments.

Overall, 78 percent of people having conventional treatment for cancer survived at least five years, compared to only 55 percent of people having alternative treatment alone. The difference was biggest for breast cancer, where people who chose alternative therapies were more than five times as likely to die within five years as those who chose conventional treatments.

Because this is an observational study, we don't know if other factors might have affected people's survival chances, as well as treatment choice. However, treatment choice seems the most likely explanation.

There are reports that some people find complementary treatments of benefit during cancer treatments. For example, some people have said that acupuncture helped them cope better with the side effects of chemotherapy.

But importantly, the emphasis is very much on the "complementary" and not on the "alternative." Ignoring medical advice on the treatment choices that potentially offer the most benefit could prove fatal.

Where Did the Story Come From?

The study was carried out by researchers from Yale School of Medicine. No funding information was provided. Two of the four researchers had received previous grants from companies involved in conventional cancer treatments, and one received research funding from the organization 21st Century Oncology.

The study was published in the peer-reviewed *Journal of the National Cancer Institute* as a "brief communication," meaning not all the study data was published. Some additional data is published online.

Most of the UK media ran reasonably accurate and balanced stories. Several – notably *The Mail Online* and *The Sun* – speculated on the types of alternative therapy people might have been using.

For example, *The Mail* said: "Breast cancer patients are 5.68 times more at risk if they opt for homeopathy." However, the researchers did not record the alternative therapies used, so we don't know whether homeopathy was one of them.

The Mail also refers to "herbs, botanicals, diets or energy crystals." While these are sometimes promoted as alternative treatments for cancer, again, we don't know which of them were used by people in this study.

What Kind of Research Was This?

This was an observational case control study. This means researchers identified people with cancer who chose to use alternative therapies (cases) and compared their outcomes with those of people with

cancer who chose conventional treatments (controls).

The controls were matched as far as possible with each case based on age, sex, demographics and type of cancer. Observational studies can show trends and links between factors (in this case between type of treatment and length of survival after cancer diagnosis) but cannot prove that one causes the other.

What Did the Research Involve?

Researchers used data from the US National Cancer Database to identify patients with breast, lung, colorectal, or prostate cancer who opted not to receive conventional cancer therapies, but were recorded as having had "other-unproven cancer treatments administered by non-medical personnel."

These patients were matched with two patients with the same type of cancer, who were similar in other ways, but had opted for conventional treatment. Researchers then looked to see how many people lived for at least five years, comparing those who chose alternative therapies with those who chose conventional cancer treatments.

Researchers only included people who had cancer that had not yet spread from the initial site. This type of cancer is usually treatable by conventional treatments. They also excluded people with stage 4 (advanced) cancer, those whose treatment was intended to be palliative rather than curative, and people whose treatment was unknown.

Researchers found 281 people who matched the criteria and who had opted for alternative therapy only. Of these, 280 were matched to 560 people with the same cancer, who chose conventional cancer treatments.

To minimise the effect of confounding factors researchers matched people in the study using these criteria:

- Cancer type
- Age
- Stage of cancer

- Health insurance – in the United States people with health insurance tend to receive a better standard of treatment
- Co-morbidities (other illnesses)
- Race
- Year of diagnosis

In addition, when calculating relative chances of surviving five years, the researchers adjusted their figures to account for the effects of medical and demographic factors.

What Were the Basic Results?

Researchers found that people choosing alternative therapies were more likely to be younger, female, have fewer other ailments, a higher cancer stage, a higher income and education level.

Taking all types of cancer together:

- 78.3 percent of people having conventional cancer treatment lived at least five years (95 percent confidence interval [CI] 74.2 percent to 81.8 percent)
- 54.7 percent of people having alternative therapies lived at least five years (95 percent CI 47.5 percent to 61.3 percent)
- People were 2.5 times more likely to live for at least five years if they had conventional treatment (hazard ratio [HR] 2.5, 95 percent CI 1.88 to 3.27)

The type of cancer made a difference, though. This is probably because some cancers can kill quickly without treatment, and treatment is very effective. We can see this in the breast cancer results:

- 86.6 percent of people who chose conventional treatment for breast cancer lived at least five years (95 percent CI 80.7 percent to 90.7 percent)
- 58.1 percent of people who chose alternative therapies for breast cancer lived at least five years (95 percent CI 46 percent to 68.5 percent)
- People were 5.68 times more likely to live at least five years if they had conventional treatment for breast cancer (HR 5.68, 95 percent CI 3.22 to 10.04)

However, for prostate cancer, it made little difference whether people opted for conventional treatment (91.5 percent lived for at least five years) or alternative treatment (86.2 percent lived for at least five years).

This is probably because prostate cancer usually grows very slowly in the early stages so few people die.

For the first five to ten years, there's little difference in those who have conventional treatments and those who have their prostate cancer monitored, with no treatment unless it starts to grow. So, you would not expect to see a difference in a five-year study.

How Did the Researchers Interpret the Results?

The researchers said: "We found that cancer patients who initially chose treatment with alternative medicine without conventional cancer treatment were more likely to die."

They added: "Improved communication between patients and caregivers, and greater scrutiny of use of alternative medicine for initial treatment of cancer is needed."

Conclusion

The results and conclusions of this study are clear: people who choose conventional treatments for cancer (such as surgery, radiotherapy, chemotherapy, and hormone treatments) are likely to live longer than those who choose alternative medicine only.

It's rare for people to choose to ignore conventional treatment completely when faced with a cancer diagnosis. More often, people choose to add complementary therapies to their conventional cancer treatment. This study doesn't apply to people combining conventional and complementary therapies.

There are some limitations to the study to be aware of:

- As an observational study, it cannot prove that treatment choice (as opposed to other factors) was the sole reason that people who chose conventional treatments lived longer. However, it seems the most likely explanation. The researchers made efforts to balance out other possibly confounding factors. It's also clear from other studies that conventional cancer therapies do work.

- The study might have misclassified some people who started taking alternative therapies when diagnosed, but switched later to conventional treatments. However, as they would be classified in this study as having taken conventional treatments, this suggests that any switchers would only strengthen the study findings, if they were reclassified as having taken alternative medicine.

People who are diagnosed with cancer and want the best chance of surviving should choose conventional cancer therapies. These give the best chance of helping people with cancer to live longer lives.

Complementary therapies such as acupuncture and tai chi may help some people but they should never take the place of potentially life-saving treatments such as chemotherapy, surgery, and radiotherapy.

EVALUATING THE AUTHOR'S ARGUMENTS:

In this viewpoint, the National Library of Medicine reports on a study of cancer survival rates considering the type of treatment used by patients. Discuss the survival rates of patients while comparing the types of treatment used and the type of cancer treated. Cite specific statistics from the viewpoint.

Viewpoint
6

Enhanced Education and Critical Thinking Skills Will Help People Reject Quackery

"I favor education over legislation, so that citizens will avoid surrendering to the charlatans due to better information and an understanding of how the real world works."

James Randi

In the following excerpted viewpoint, James Randi maintains that a lack of adequate science education and critical thinking skills allow quackery to flourish. The author urges readers to be aware that although his thoughts and words are from nineteen years ago, the situation has not changed noticeably in that there is still no proof of supernatural powers and that fakes are still fakes. Rather than counting on governments to protect citizens through legislation, we should focus on education and the power of critical thinking. For over forty years, James Randi has been a well-known skeptic in the business of "outing" fakes of all kinds.

"James Randi on Quackery and the Need for Science Education," by James Randi, The Skeptics Society. Reprinted by permission.

1. What does the public need to be protected from according to Randi?
2. What statistics about smoking leads Randi to report that the public has not been successfully educated?
3. Identify the three examples of quackery reported by the author.

This is not the first time that a conjuror has addressed members of the Congress. The justly famous Harry Houdini appeared before a packed House in 1926 to promote an anti-fortunetelling bill that was highly unpopular with the seers and mountebanks of that day. Houdini, as I, was dismayed at the public belief in supernatural forces and pseudoscientific notions. But perhaps his solution—legislation—was not the ideal one. I rather favor education over legislation, so that citizens will avoid surrendering to the charlatans due to better information and an understanding of how the real world works. There is no mightier weapon than education.

On the internet, in television commercials, in fact via all the media, the American people are being offered merchandise, medical systems, financial services, and investment plans. That pursuit of opportunity on the part of the entrepreneur is what we call "The American Way," and we must applaud originality and an applied work ethic, of course. But when business becomes hucksterism, the public needs to be protected. How valid are these offers that promise instant weight loss, renewed vitality, overnight youth, and cures for everything from high cholesterol to poor circulation? And how can we educate young people to judge these claims?

Medical Quackery

Let me give you just one example of the sort of nonsense with which we have to deal. Major drug chains across the United States are now offering, as part of their off-the-shelf cure-alls, homeopathic preparations that have zero content! Now, I'll not go into my usual tirade on the worthlessness of this ancient notion called homeopathy, but will

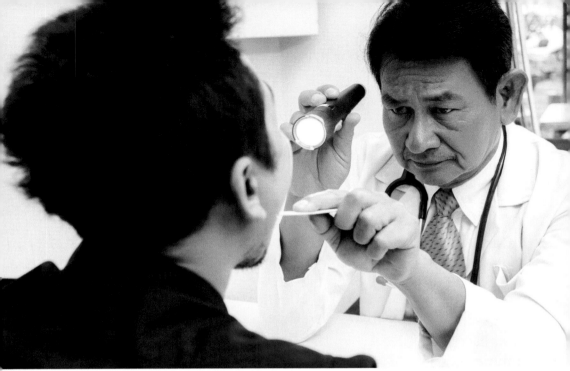

It is important to be educated and think critically when evaluating medical treatments and practitioners. If something seems too good to be true, it usually is.

offer you a brief example or two of what it really is. First, a demonstration. I hold in my hand a package that purports to be a cure for "insomnia." It is a remedy sold by one of the major nationwide drug chains, and the label instructs me to take a maximum dose of "one tablet every two hours." I'll do better than that. There are forty-five tablets here. I'll take the whole works.

What have I just taken? Well, the list of ingredients I see on the back of this box lists "silver nitrate, 6x." I must tell you that silver nitrate is a caustic, deadly poison, and I've just taken more than twenty-two times the maximum dose of this material! But the major ingredient listed on this sleep-inducing medication is "coffee." Coffee? Yes, because, you see, homeopathy works in just the opposite way that "regular" medicine works. But just how much coffee did I get when I ingested all forty-five of the pills in this package? Zero. In fact, the concentration of "30x"—the favored concentration in most homeopathy—would mean that there is one part of coffee in one thousand, billion, billion, billion parts of milk sugar. As my good friend and physicist Bob Park has pointed out, that means we would have to eat sixteen swimming pools filled to the brim with these pills in order to get just one molecule of caffeine into our systems! [...] The point of this demonstration is not to prove that homeopathic compounds are safe—they certainly are—but to show you that they are useless.

Government Leadership

And where is the USFDA? Standing with their hands tied, I suspect. That agency is well aware that stores are selling this quackery, but they can do nothing because the quackery was here before the agency existed, and it's "grandfathered" in, fully immune and protected from examination and regulation. In regard to doubtful weight-loss schemes being offered via infomercials, I must say that the FDA has recently put into effect a requirement for strong disclaimers in the promotional material—though no requirements that actual clinical tests have established the efficacy of the products offered. Endless testimonials do not establish validity. Much to their credit, the FTC has come down on the purveyors of the so-called "vitamin O" scam just recently. Asked about the enforcement efforts of the FTC, spokesperson Michelle Rusk replied, "...we can't get every problem that's out there." That simply should not be the case.

But—and this is my major point here—a properly educated and informed public would know about this, and protective laws would not be required. Again, education is the key. A recent survey conducted through the *Journal of the American Medical Association* showed that of current smokers, only 29 percent believed that they were at higher-than-average risk for heart attack, and only 40 percent thought they were more likely to develop cancer. That's incredible, and shows that we have not successfully educated the public to understand and accept factual discoveries made by science. Misinformation, purposely and effectively distributed through the internet, has led to the belief that anthrax vaccinations cause cancer and sterility, even death. Armed forces personnel have been demoted or dismissed from the forces, for refusing to accept the ordered immunity measures, and others have resigned commissions rather than be treated. And this is for a disease that is invariably fatal, and is easily contracted by simple inhalation. The truth about the vaccination process has fallen on deaf or merely uneducated ears.

The words "natural," and "herbal," are seen and heard aplenty in advertisements for quack products. Herbal panaceas and magnetic devices have re-emerged from the uninformed 1800s into the present world. They've taken on a new gloss by the use of terms such as "quantum physics" and "new science." And US citizens, some seventy million of them, are embracing untested and unproven nostrums. We owe them better than to ignore their need for information. No one can dispute the proven value of herbal substances in medicine; they've been used effectively for centuries now. Indeed, herbals are a solid base from which a majority of our working remedies are obtained. But we must first evaluate, and second standardize, these materials before putting them on the market.

[...]

One Million Dollars Is Offered

If the US public had a better understanding of astronomy than they do of astrology, if they knew more about numbers than about numerology, they would be better able to defend themselves against the charlatans who function freely in the United States, unafraid of the consequences. As a case in point, you might recall a device called "The Stimulator," which was sold on TV infomercials by Lee Meriwether, a former Miss America, and Evel Knievel, the daredevil motorcyclist. It was a plastic gimmick that made a snapping noise, and was said to relieve aches and pains. The FTC finally closed down that operation, but only after they'd been on the air for more than three years. The maximum fine was imposed, $40,000, but after bringing in millions, I hardly think that the promoters cared very much.

Science Education

The public's understanding of science is weak. A large percentage of those who regularly scoff at the progress science has made would simply not be here if it were not for advances in our understanding of the world around us (and I am an excellent example of that fact) and that is exactly what science is all about. Science is part of our survival mechanism, it works, and it can be shown to work. The quacks and scam artists out there do not have a record of success, and leave behind them broken hearts, crippled bodies, and shattered dreams.

A recent National Science Foundation survey shows that, although an overwhelming number of Americans support scientific research and government sponsorship of the same, half of the Americans surveyed were unable to answer fundamental science questions about the world around them. Historically, there has been a close relationship among perception, misperception based on "apparent" reality, and scientific knowledge derived from critical analysis. An education in the process of critical thinking investigating why we think what we think, trains students to examine the gaps and inconsistencies in their knowledge base, and to more accurately separate fact from fantasy.

The U.S. Patent Office, at one time, issued patents only after a working model of a proposed device or system had been produced. Regularly today, plans for perpetual motion and free-energy machines, cheap-and-easy counterfeit money detectors, control systems triggered by thought waves, and devices that find drugs, guns, minerals, and oil, are received by the office. Are working examples still required by the office? No. It now seems that all that is needed is for a "master" to look over the application, and rubber-stamp it.

I hold in my hand a device that many of you will have run into when you tried to spend a $50 or $100 bill. It's called "The Counterfeit Detector Pen." The makers claim that a phony bill stroked by this pen will register a black line, while a genuine bill will show an amber-colored line. And it bears U.S. Patent Number 5,063,163. The patent examiner who approved this patent read that counterfeiters would use cheap recycled paper, which has starch content, and since this is an iodine pen, the cheap paper would turn black, as starch does when in contact with iodine. Do you really think that a counterfeiter would use cheap paper to print on, folks? Of course not. But this pen has made a lot of folks very happy. First, we have those who sell the pen, by the hundreds of thousands in major office supply houses. Second, even happier, are the counterfeiters themselves, whose product will never show up this way, and will go right back into circulation. And who pays for this? We do. We allow, by this means, some hundreds of millions of dollars in bogus bills to circulate freely, since countless restaurants, stores, and other businesses in this country depend upon this device—this quite useless pen—to decide whether they should accept a currency bill. This is costing money!

I'm all for simple experimentation. Here I have a $50 bill. I suspect this bill might be counterfeit. Sir, please take the Counterfeit Detector Pen and in accordance with the instructions, stroke a line upon an open portion of the face of the bill. What is the result? That means the bill is genuine, according to the patent papers, which states, "a light golden-brown colored test area will indicate the presence of genuine paper currency." Please turn the bill over and tell us what you see there. (The bill is a photocopy made on newsprint.)

Ladies and gentlemen, we like to believe that we're sophisticated and aware. That we can't be fooled. But we're human beings, with all the failings of our species. Customs agents, police officers, legislators, patent examiners, even scientists and technicians, are all subject to bad judgement from time to time. It's inevitable. But much of that weakness can be avoided by education at an early age. We owe it to our kids to inform them and train them how to think, not what to think. In many ways, we've failed this generation. Let's not allow ourselves to be taken advantage of anymore. We can and must oppose those who would cheat us.

In my work, I've seen firsthand the ravages of superstition and misinformation. It's appalling, I can tell you: kids who have checked out of reality and adopted fantasies rather than facts; adults who have abandoned any efforts at improving themselves and want to hire gurus to run their lives.

My heroes are few but large. Carl Sagan was a good friend. Isaac Asimov was close to me in many ways. Martin Gardner is a minor god of mine. Richard Feynman and I exchanged many useful thoughts. And Richard Dawkins has supported me and the James Randi Education Foundation in many ways. But heroes should be more abundant.

Lest you get any notion that this dependence upon nonsense is new to us, let me read you a quotation:

Heroes have gone out; quacks have come in;
The reign of quacks has not ended with this century;
The scepter is held with a firmer grasp;
Their empire has a wider boundary.
We are all the slaves of quackery in one shape or another.

That was spoken by Thomas Carlyle, a prominent philosopher and historian, in the year 1881, 118 years ago. We are, it seems, reliving a bad aspect of our own history. We should learn from that, and put an end to it.

EVALUATING THE AUTHOR'S ARGUMENTS:

In this viewpoint, James Randi cites facts from a then recent National Science Foundation survey that found that about half of those Americans surveyed were unable to answer fundamental science questions about the world around them. How does this affect the ability of charlatans and con artists? Use specific details from one of the scams cited by Randi to support your claims.

Facts About Alternative Medicine

Editor's note: These facts can be used in reports to add credibility when making important points or claims.

Important Definitions:
- Complementary Medicine: (NCCIH) Medical treatments combining non-Western practices with conventional medicine.
- Alternative Medicine: (NCCIH) Non-Western practice used solely and in place of conventional medicine.
- Randomized controlled trials (RCTs): The most rigorous—also called gold standard— testing method by researchers on potential preventive, diagnostic, and therapeutic medical intervention.
- Placebo effect: (NCCIH) A beneficial result to health from a person's anticipation that some treatment—pill, procedure, or injection, for example—will help them.

Five Forms of CAM (according to NCCIH)
- Whole medical system: traditional Chinese medicine, homeopathy, naturopathy, Ayurveda
- Mind-body therapies: music and art therapy, meditation, prayer
- Biologically based therapies: dietary and herbal supplements
- Manipulative therapies: chiropractic or osteopathic manipulation
- Energy therapies: tai chi, Reiki, therapeutic touch, qigong, electromagnetic therapy

First Medicines
- First natural product: Morphine, a pure, natural product was marketed in 1826.
- First part natural/part synthetic product: Aspirin, a partly natural, partly synthesized product was marketed by Bayer in 1899.
- Potential plant sources: Approximately 35,000-70,000 different

plant species have been investigated for their potential possibilities for medical products.

- Ten most common CAM: (in order from highest percentage used to lowest) Natural products (17.7 percent), deep breathing (10.9 percent), yoga/tai chi/qigong (10.1 percent), chiropractic or osteopathic manipulation (8.4 percent), meditation (8.0 percent), massage (6.9 percent), special diets (3.0 percent), homeopathy (2.2 percent), progressive relaxation (2.1 percent), guided imagery (1.7 percent)
- WHO list: 252 drugs are considered to be basic and essential to provide health coverage.

Statistics

- Over 30 percent of US adults use health care treatments not part of conventional Western medicine.
- About 12 percent of US children use health care treatments not part of conventional Western medicine.
- Almost 20 percent of US adults use natural products—other than vitamins or minerals—such as herbs or probiotics. Fish oil is one of the most commonly used supplements.
- About 80 percent of the world's population uses traditional or herbal medicine according to WHO.

Organizations to Contact

The editors have compiled the following list of organizations concerned with the issues debated in this book. The descriptions are derived from materials provided by the organizations. All have publications or information available for interested readers. The list was compiled on the date of publication of the present volume; the information provided here may change. Be aware that many organizations take several weeks or longer to respond to inquiries, so allow as much time as possible for the receipt of requested materials.

American Alternative Medical Association (AAMA)
2200 Market St., Suite 803 Galveston, TX 77550-1530
(888) 764-2237
email: office@joinaama.com
website: www.joinaama.com/default.asp
AAMA is dedicated to promoting a positive image of practitioners of traditional and nontraditional therapies.

Cleveland Clinic
9500 Euclid Ave. Cleveland, Oho, 44195
(800) 223-2273
website: https://my.clevelandclinic.org
As one of the largest hospital systems in the United States, the Cleveland Clinic analyzes a wide array of topics within the field of complementary and alternative medicine on its website.

Mayo Clinic
200 First St. SW Rochester, MN, 55905
(507) 284-2511
website: www.mayoclinic.org
Number 1 rated hospital system in the United States. Dedicated to expert health care specializing in complex health issues and treatments. Its online Mayo Clinic News Network provides a large resource for information on health issues.

National Center for Complementary and Integrative Health
9000 Rockville Pike, Bethesda, Maryland, 20892
(888) 644-6226
email: info@nccih.nih.gov
website: www.nccih.nih.gov
NCCIH is the US federal agency dedicated to scientific research on the health practices and treatments not considered part of Western conventional medicine. NCCIH works to find which alternative and complementary treatments actually are effective and safe.

National Institutes of Health (NIH)
9000 Rockville Pike, Bethesda, Maryland, 20892
(301) 496-4000
email: NIHinfo@od.nih.gov
website: www.nih.gov
The medical research arm of the United States, the NIH is dedicated to discoveries that improve and save lives. Search the website and find a trove of information concerning the topic of complementary and alternative medicine.

PhRMA Foundation
950 F Street, NW, Suite 300, Washington, DC, 20004
(202) 572-7756
email: foundation@phrma.org
website: www.phrmafoundation.org/
PhRMA Foundation is dedicated to helping young scientists pursue careers in research, development, and education related to the discovery of pharmaceuticals.

US Department of Agriculture (USDA)
1400 Independence Ave., SW, Washington, DC, 20250
(202) 720-2791
website: www.usda.gov
A US governmental agency, the USDA website provides links to information about health, research, clinical trials, and the latest news and statistics on complementary and alternative medicine.

US National Library of Medicine (NLM)
8600 Rockville Pike, Bethesda, Maryland, 20894
(888) 346-3656
website: www.nlm.nih.gov
Maintains and makes available a vast print and electronic information resource. Millions of people around the globe make use of this, the world's largest biomedical library, for billions of searches on an enormous range of health topics and issues.

World Health Organization (WHO)
Avenue Appia 20, 1202 Geneva
+41-22-7912111
website: http://www.who.int/
Provides leadership by coordinating and directing international health and health concerns within the United Nations' system. In cooperation with signatory nations, the WHO regulates and researches a wide array of issues dealing with complementary and alternative medicine concerns and maintains a corresponding number of publications.

For Further Reading

Books

Bausell, R. Barker. *Snake Oil Science: The Truth About Complementary and Alternative Medicine.* New York, NY: Oxford University Press, 2007.

Researched and written by a biostatistician, this book takes a long hard look at the alternative medicine industry and serves up conclusions found by others. Any positive effects are short-term placebo effects, not cures.

Borins, Mel. *A Doctor's Guide to Alternative Medicine: What Works, What Doesn't, and Why.* Guilford, CT: Lyons Press, 2014.

Resource that provides thorough information about scientifically tested alternative therapies. Written by a doctor, for consumers and other doctors seeking accurate information about alternative treatments to use in tandem with conventional medicine.

Brown, Candy Gunther. *The Healing Gods: Complementary and Alternative Medicine in Christian America.* New York, NY: Oxford University Press, 2013.

Examines complementary and alternative medicine from a Christian viewpoint. Chapters give a religious bent to CAM, and address yoga, chiropractors, acupuncture, and more.

Cardoza, Steven. *Chinese Holistic Medicine in Your Daily Life: Combine Acupressure, Herbal Remedies & Qigong for Integrated Natural Healing.* Woodbury, MN: Llewellyn Publications, 2017.

Overview of Chinese holistic medicine which looks at Qi, the energy of life, yin and yang, acupressure, Chinese herbs and herbal formulas.

Larson, Christine A. *Alternative Medicine.* Westport, CT: Greenwood Press, 2007.

Provides an introduction to the topic of alternative medicine and its origins, theories, and business. Also investigates whether alternative medicine works, why consumers use the treatments, and if pharmaceuticals work better than alternate treatments.

Meadows, Susannah. *The Other Side of Impossible: Ordinary People Who Faced Daunting Medical Challenges and Refused to Give Up.* New York, NY: Random House, 2017.

Details true stories of people up against terribly challenging medical conditions. By using untraditional treatments and perseverance along with the powerful mind-body connection they triumphed over their medical illness.

Offit, Paul A. M.D. *Do You Believe in Magic? The Sense and Nonsense of Alternative Medicine.* New York, NY: Harper, 2013.

Exposes the alternative medicine industry and its treatments as problematic, ineffective, and sometimes deadly. Admits that some very popular alternative therapies provide help for some conditions due to the placebo effect.

Shapiro, Nina. M.D. *HYPE: A Doctor's Guide to Medical Myths, Exaggerated Claims and Bad Advice—How to Tell What's Real and What's Not.* New York, NY: St. Martin's Press, 2018.

Details information on a wide range of current medical myths and modern hype. Includes information about complementary and alternative medical treatments, vaccinations, vitamin supplements, medical jargon and testing, and other popular topics.

Weil, Andrew, M.D. *Mind Over Meds: Know When Drugs are Necessary, When Alternatives are Better—and When to Let Your Body Heal on Its Own.* New York, NY: Little, Brown and Company, 2017.

Written by a prominent doctor in the integrative medicine movement, this book is a valuable resource on the commonly prescribed medicines, why they may or may not be effective, and if possible are other alternative treatments effective, safe, and warranted.

Periodicals and Internet Sources

Altshul, Sara, "Why a Growing Number of Mainstream Doctors are Making Herbs Their Go-To Remedies," *Prevention,* September 15, 2014. https://www.prevention.com/life/a20464999/more-doctors-prescribing-herbal-supplements-and-natural-remedies/.

Andrews, Betsy, "I Healed Myself Inside By Spending More Time Outside," *Prevention*, July 2017. https://www.prevention.com/life/a20477692/i-healed-myself-inside-by-spending-more-time-outside/.

Brechka, Nicole, "Green Foods Health Benefits," *Better Nutrition,* April 1, 2018. https://www.betternutrition.com/features-dept/green-foods-health-benefits.

Breeding, Ashley, "3 Best Natural Migraine Remedies," *Prevention,* November 20, 2017. https://www.prevention.com/health/a20506093/3-best-natural-migraine-remedies/.

Christensen, Jen, "A Third of Americans Use Alternative Medicine," CNN, February 11, 2015. https://www.cnn.com/2015/02/11/health/feat-alternative-medicine-study/index.html.

Coutre, Lydia, "Former Cleveland Clinic Docs Self-Fund New Functional Medicine Practice," *Cleveland Business,* March 4, 2018. http://www.crainscleveland.com/article/20180304/news/153736/former-cleveland-clinic-docs-self-fund-new-functional-medicine-practice.

Dunkin, Mary Ann, "The New Integration," *Georgia Trend*, June 2017. http://www.georgiatrend.com/June-2017/The-New-Integration/.

Dworkin, Ronald W., "Science, Faith, and Alternative Medicine," Hoover Institution, August 1, 2001. https://www.hoover.org/research/science-faith-and-alternative-medicine.

Evans, Joanna, "Natural Vs. Medical—Acupuncture Vs. Sleeping Pills for Insomnia," *What Doctors Don't Tell You,* August 2016. https://www.wddty.com/magazine/2016/august/natural-vs-medical-acupuncture-vs-sleeping-pills-for-insomnia.html.

Krainin, Todd, and Slade, Stephanie, "The Alternative Medicine Racket," *Reason,* December 2015. https://reason.com/archives/2015/12/01/the-alternative-medicine-racke.

Krigman, Eliza, "Go Wild: My Month as a Hunter-Gatherer—and How it Affected My Health," *Marie Claire,* December 15, 2014. https://www.marieclaire.com/culture/news/a12801/go-wild/.

Oster, Lauren, "Acupuncture for Your Cat? What to Know About Alternative Medicine for Your Pet," *Health,* April 27, 2017. http://www.health.com/pets/alternative-medicine-for-pet.

Pfaff, Leslie Garisto, "As Addiction Rises, Doctors Seek Pain-Relieving Alternatives to Opioids," *New Jersey Monthly,* November 1, 2017.

Reno, Jaime, "Alternative Medicine Finally Becoming More Mainstream," *Healthline,* April 2016. https://www.healthline.com/health-news/alternative-medicine-becoming-mainstream#1.

Ridderbusch, Katja, "Opioid Crisis Forces Physicians to Focus On Alternative Pain Treatments," *WABE,* December 15, 2017. https://www.wabe.org/opioid-crisis-forces-physicians-focus-alternative-pain-treatments/.

Schenker, Matthew, "Integrative Veterinary Care for Your Animal," *Canadian Dogs,* June 2, 2014. https://canadiandogs.com/stay-close-with-your-pets-vet/.

Turner, Lisa, "Prevent, Treat & Recover: A Flu Guide," *Better Nutrition*, December 31, 2016. https://www.betternutrition.com/features-dept/prevent-treat-recover-a-flu-guide.

Weiss, Jean, "9 Natural Remedies Doctors Trust," *Prevention,* July 17, 2015. https://www.prevention.com/health/a20470029/natural-cures-you-can-trust/.

Websites

Consumer Reports (www.consumerreports.org/cro/2012/04/alternative-treatments/index.htm)

Using a survey of over forty-five thousand subscribers, Consumer Reports tallies the experiences from various alternative therapies and treatments used by people. Everything from allergy treatments to yoga, presented in easy-to-read statistics with further links to extra information on complementary and alternative medicine.

Kids Health (kidshealth.org/)

Comprehensive site on health for kids. Includes links for parents, educators, kids, and teens. Search the site for information about complementary and alternative medicine.

NIH—National Center for Complementary and Integrative Health (nccih.nih.gov/health/children)

The NIH provides a wealth of information about complementary and health approaches for children. Easy-to-read charts show the most common complementary treatments used for children, and the most common childhood diseases or conditions when complementary medicine treatment is used.

Index

A

acupuncture, 7, 13, 14, 15, 19, 25, 47, 50, 55, 56, 95, 99
Adams, Jon, 76
Albright, Logan, 27
alternative medicine, 7–9, 11–40, 42–74, 76–79, 81–83, 85–88, 89–92, 93–99, 100–107
  changes to the practice of, 76–79, 80–83, 84–88, 89–92, 93–99, 100–107
  differences from conventional medicine, 11–15, 16–20, 21–26, 27–30, 31–35, 36–40
  does it help or harm, 42–47, 48–51, 53–58, 59–62, 63–68, 69–74
  funding for research, 81–83, 85–88
anti-science sentiments, 28–30
aromatherapy, 25, 84, 85
astrology, 85, 104
autism, 53–58, 92
Ayurvedic medicine, 7, 23, 25, 33, 90

B

Bassett, Deborah R., 16
biofeedback, 25
breast cancer, 67, 68, 94, 95, 97

C

complementary and alternative medicine (CAM), 22–24
  efficacy, 24–25
  examples of, 25–26
cancer treatments, 93
  alternative therapy, 50–51, 65–68, 69–72, 96–99
  chemotherapy, 50, 60, 65, 70–74, 94–95, 98–99
  conventional treatments, 64–65, 72–74, 93–95, 96
Centers for Disease Control and Prevention (CDC), 8
chiropractic medicine, 25, 56, 77
Chopra, Deepak, 90–92
clinical trials, 24–25, 51, 66, 70, 72, 81–83, 85–88
conventional medicine, 7–9, 12, 17–20, 22, 24, 29, 45, 59, 61, 63–65, 70
  effectiveness of, 64–65
crystals, 60, 95

D

Daily Mail, 84, 95
Daniels, Scott, 63
Dawkins, Richard, 90, 106
detoxification, 46, 56
diet therapy, 25, 46, 54–55, 56–58, 66–68, 71, 95

E
Eastern mysticism, 85–86
Ernst, Edzard, 42, 59, 72

F
faith healing, 85–86
FTC, 103, 104

G
Gorski, David, 85–87
Gottseen, Joel, 89

H
Health Canada, 31, 34, 35
herbal medicine, 13, 15, 18, 23,
    25, 32, 33, 70, 72–74, 104
HIE Help Center, 21
holistic medicine movement,
    14–15, 17, 23, 45–46, 56,
    87–88, 90
homeopathy, 25, 84, 85, 87, 90,
    95, 101–103
Houdini, Harry, 101
Hughes, Joanna, 11
hypnosis, 25

I
integrative medicine, 7, 12, 17,
    23–24, 55, 56–57, 87

J
James Randi Education
    Foundation, 106
Jobs, Steve, 69–71, 74
*Journal of the American Medical
    Association*, 103
*Journal of the National Cancer
    Institute*, 95

K
Katz, David, 56, 57
Knievel, Evel, 104
Komesaroff, Paul, 36

L
Levinovitz, Alan, 53

M
massage therapy, 25, 77
meditation, 7, 23, 25, 70
Meriwether, Lee, 104
Minchin, Tim, 92
miracle cures, 8–9, 53–58
misinformation, 103–104, 106

N
National Center for
    Complementary and
    Integrative Health (NCCIH),
    7–8, 12, 23
National Library of
    Medicine, 93
National Science
    Foundation, 105
natural health products
    (NHP), 32–35
    risks from, 33–35
naturopathy, 7, 15, 23, 25
New Age, 90, 91
Novella, Steven, 85–88

O
osteopathic manipulative ther-
    apy (OMT), 23, 25

P
Perlman, Adam

(director of Duke's Integrative Medicine), 57
placebo effect, 8–9, 29, 72, 89, 91–92
prostate cancer, 98–99
pseudoscience, 38, 84, 86–87

Q
qigong, 7, 26
quackery, 42–47, 85–88, 89–92, 100–103, 104–107
Quantum Healing, 90

R
Randi, James, 100
reflexology, 15, 26, 45
Reiki, 15, 24, 26, 56, 84, 85–88
Reiki Council, 87–88
Ryan, Sandra, 69

S
Scholey, Andrew, 80
science education, 39, 104–107
scientific method, 92
sugar pill, 71, 91

T
tai chi, 7, 14, 26, 99
traditional Chinese medicine (TCM), 7, 11, 13, 14, 15, 23, 26
traditional medicine, 8, 17, 33
21st Century Oncology, 95

U
U.S. Patent Office, 105
USFDA, 103

V
vaccination, 28, 92, 103
vitamins, 7, 32, 33, 54, 63, 67, 68, 70, 103

W
Western vs. complementary medicine, 38–39
World Health Organization (WHO), 8,

Y
Yale School of Medicine, 85, 95
yoga, 7, 15, 26

Picture Credits

Cover Blackday/Shutterstock.com; p. 10 Kerdkanno/Shutterstock.com; p. 12 Tom Wang/Shutterstock.com; p. 18 Steve Debenport/E+/Getty Images; p. 22 Juri Pozzi/Shutterstock.com; p. 28 adriaticfoto/Shutterstock.com; p. 32 Paul Colangelo/National Geographic Magazines/Getty Images; p. 37 AshTproductions/Shutterstock.com; p. 41 Lucky Business/Shutterstock.com; p. 43 Science Photo Library/Alamy Stock Photo; p. 49 George Rudy/Shutterstock.com; p. 54 BSIP SA/Alamy Stock Photo; p. 60 Michael Bann/Shutterstock.com; p. 64 Tim Masters/Shutterstock.com; p. 71 Rick Smolan/Getty Images; p. 75 Andrey Popov/Shutterstock.com; p. 77 Billion Photos/Shutterstock.com; p. 81 Photofusion/Universal Images Group/Getty Images; p. 86 Christopher Bissell/The Image Bank/Getty Images; p. 91 tongcom photographer/Shutterstock.com; p. 94 Bildagentur-online/Universal Images Group/Getty Images; p. 102 2p2play/Shutterstock.com